Guilty 'Til Proven Innocent

by

James C. Reynolds

DEDICATION

To my mother, Lorene B. Reynolds, who, at 85 pounds, has got to be the strongest woman I know. Her indomitable spirit, unassailable fortitude and insurmountable stubbornness make her a great example of a Godly saint and Soldier of the Cross.

FOREWARD

In the winter of 2004, Jim Reynolds was accused of a crime he did not commit. He was originally under suspicion for allegedly operating a child pornography website on his computer and ultimately charged with twelve counts of possessing child pornography.

Mr. Reynolds was arrested and incarcerated for three days, and after making bail, he endured over two years of waiting until the charges were finally dismissed in the summer of 2006.

His story is one of extreme identity theft accomplished by the shrewdest of cyberspace criminals. A person in Cincinnati, Ohio, hacked into Mr. Reynolds personal computer in late 2003 and obtained one of his credit card numbers, which had been used to make a computer purchase for business related purposes. The thief then created a child pornography website using Jim's credit card number and utilized his personal computer to send e-mails to subscribers. The resulting prosecution nearly cost Jim Reynolds not only his personal liberty but his very life.

In a very readable account, he describes in great detail the shock and anguish of incarceration and accompanying loss of dignity. From the death threats at the jail, which led to solitary confinement, to the shunning behavior of former friends and associates, the author relates his agonizing journey from accusation to exoneration.

What happened to Jim Reynolds can happen to anyone who owns a personal computer anywhere in the world. The murky world of internet fraud is misunderstood and underestimated by most computer owners. Most of us have heard of hacking, computer viruses and spam, but what about <u>Worms</u>, <u>Sporn</u>, <u>Crackers</u> and <u>Trojan Horses</u>. The latter are among the most insidious of methods used to infiltrate the computers of unwary victims.

Legislation to combat fraudulent computer activity is being undertaken by the U.S. government as well as various states. In some cases, like Mr. Reynolds', the attempted prosecution is frantically undertaken and is conducted without decorum or consideration for the rights, feelings or reputation of the defendant. Moreover, the media frenzy that ultimately accompanies such a prosecution all but destroys the reputation of the accused. The media pressure compels the authorities to zealously pursue the case, even when the evidence is insufficient to convict. One wonders how often such prosecutorial blackmail is attempted in the State's effort to save face.

Mr. Reynolds devotes a significant portion of the book to educating the reader to the potential dangers lurking in the world of cyberspace and to developing various strategies for discovering, confronting and eliminating computer fraud and identity theft.

Jim Reynolds has weathered his storm. He has been through the fire and emerged (almost) unscathed to tell his story. His temperament is one of abiding faith and trust in the Almighty to deliver him from the clutches of evil. The result is a powerful story of one mans personal struggle against adversity and false accusations.

Former Judge Hyrum O. Pierce

Hon. Hyrum O. Pierce is a former Superior Court Judge for Rockdale County, Georgia. He is a practicing attorney-at-law with offices within sight of Rockdale County Courthouse in Conyers, Georgia.

CAST OF CHARACTERS

THE ACCUSED ....James C. (Jim/Jimmy) Reynolds
THE ASSOCIATE .... Sean Peacock
THE CHAIRMAN ....Dr. James D. Harper
THE DOCTOR .... Dr. Jerry A. Patterson
THE FRIEND .... Donald K. (Joe) Patterson
THE NEIGHBOR ....Linda Baker
THE OFFICE MANAGER..............Debbie B. Boyd
THE SISTER .... Beverly R. Martin
THE WIFE.................................. Alison V. Reynolds

ACKNOWLEDGEMENTS

A project of this nature involves more than just the author—it involves a host of people who contributed to the story in some fashion. No matter how minute the contribution, each and every one deserves appreciation and thanks. I hope I don't forget anyone, but if I do it is not from a lack of appreciation, but simply the result of a poor memory and creeping old age.

I want to first express my highest praise for my Lord and Savior, Jesus Christ. He is the reason for the whole book. I wish to thank his representative on earth, Dr. Jerry A. Patterson and his wife, Sally. Thank you seems insufficient for all you both have done.

Many thanks goes to my mother, Lorene B. Reynolds; my "big sister," Beverly Martin and my brother-in-law, Carl Martin; their children and their families, Chuck and Wendy Martin, Kelvin and Sherri Poole, and Scott and Sue Martin. To my children, Joy Myers and her husband, Tommy Myers; Jenna Reynolds and their mother, Jennifer C. Reynolds. To my step-children, who have become like my own, AJ Rolling and his wife, Maggie Rolling and their daughter, Misty Jane Rolling (and also to the one on the way), Robert George Rolling and Virginia Etta Rolling and their father, Jim Rolling and his wife, Carol Rolling. I appreciate my mother-in-law, Jane Broome and her children and their families; Debbie Boyd and her husband, JB, Julie Rubenfeld and Jamie Broome.

I truly appreciate my attorney and his wife, Garland and Irene Moore; Former Judge Hyrum Pierce; Attorney and State Representative Robert Mumford; and my neighbors, Ed and Linda Baker. Some special friends include Chris Westlake, Larry Chestnut, Marty Ross and Larry Pirkle, Robert Diggle, Dawn and Zack of the Bibb County Record Room and all of the legal researchers, title searchers, attorneys and clerks in the Metro-Atlanta and Georgia Courthouses.

I wish to give a "God bless ya'll" to all of the members of Faith Tabernacle United Pentecostal Church of Conyers, GA, especially to the families of Joe Patterson, Keith Patterson, Joe Fagler, Anne Bailey, Rev. Michael Patterson, Ricky Patterson, Danny Knarr, Dr. James Harper, Steve Hardy, Denise Martin, Steve Cronan, Johnny Mathis, Ryan Mathis, Eugene Stovall, John Kendall, Rev. Shannon Peacock, John Elrod, Rev. Ashley Neal, Sean Peacock, Bo Chandler, Jay Barwick, Steve Rosser, Chuck Feaselman, Margie Shepherd, Kenny French, Rev. Ed Horne, Judy Reeves, Mary Wright, Rev. Richard Shorter, Wayne Reynolds, Bobby Eskew,

Martha Sullivan, Woody Hudson, Chris Reeves, Karen Lewis, Arlee Boggin, Jake McClure, Sandra McClure, Wade Owen, Anthony Reynolds, Floyd Shorter, Rhonda Landry, Tom Marszalek, Wray Stewart, Roy Collins, Truman Cronan, Rev. Clell Eskew, Lee Eskew, the late Eddie Martin, and all of the others I just don't have room to name.

I wish to thank my editor and manager, Stephanie Barwick—you've kept me on the right track, inspired me to finish this book and made sure it was as complete as possible. Any mistakes, errors or omissions are solely my responsibility. And a great big 'thank you' to my wife, Alison Virginia Reynolds—you know I have really appreciated and enjoyed the handy Diet-Coke dispenser in my library that you gave me.

James C. Reynolds
November 2006

INTRODUCTION

On a cold wintry day in January, 2004, my world was literally invaded by an attack of Satan that almost destroyed my mind, my emotions, and my life. This is the story of that horrible two and a half year ordeal and how God, using many and various resources, delivered me through the most trying time of my life. By the time this story ends, you will feel the roller-coaster ride that I was on, with my family and friends hanging on to it with me.

For a whole story to be known and understood, it is best to present the most perspectives accessible. Understandably, any individual perspective is limited to the point of view available. For instance, one individual may describe a train rolling down the tracks by saying, "The train traveled from my left to the right." While just across on the other side of the tracks, another individual's perspective would be described by, "The train traveled from my right to the left." Same train, same track, and same time of travel-just a different perspective presented.

In this story, the charges brought against me can be represented by the train engine pulling the boxcars full of allegations behind it. It is steaming down the tracks of justice. On the left hand side of the tracks, law enforcement, represented by the prosecuting attorneys, says, "The train is traveling from my left to the right, and Jim Reynolds is guilty." Standing on the right hand side of the tracks is the law represented by my defense attorney, who says, "The train is traveling from my right to the left, and Jim Reynolds is innocent." Same train, same track, and same time of travel-but different perspectives. Only, those aren't the only perspectives available. There's the point of view, my perspective, of standing in the middle of the tracks while the train bears down on me! A totally different and unique point of view and perspective, I assure you.

And the train is probably painted orange.

Always orange.

Thankfully, the Master Conductor took control of the train and delivered me, just in time.

In the beginning, my narrative tells of the investigation into the allegations that I was the owner and operator of a child pornography website. As the story unfolds, you will find that not only were my family and I victims of a hostile takeover of our computers by a person or persons unknown, but my identity was stolen and used to commit this most horrendous and terrible crime. Even after the evidence showed that I was not responsible for the creation of the website, I was still arrested and charged with possession of child pornography because of images found on my computers. Significantly, the images were the result of either spam or a virus, but this took quite some time to prove. In fact, it was two and a half years before all charges were dropped and the case was dismissed.

My family and I suffered the humiliation and shame of having front-page newspaper coverage, radio broadcasts and television telecasts (including CNN) sensationalize my arrest, thus creating in the minds of many people that I was guilty 'til proven innocent. The major focus of the narrative involves the myriad of emotions that I felt throughout the length of this ordeal and how I was brought through the situation by the mighty hand of God.

You will not find antagonism, animosity or criticism of the jail or justice systems in here. You will not find any complaints or antagonism toward law enforcement officials, judges or District Attorneys. All of these serve the vital interests of our communities and societies and are worthy of praise for the sacrifices they give in performing oftentimes thankless tasks. These people attempt to fulfill their oaths to protect their communities from the criminal elements that permeate every level of society. I cannot spiritually afford to carry any bitterness or animosity.

You will find the stories of people who performed the most simple of activities, yet their efforts turned out to be a tremendous contribution to my welfare and emotions. Some of these folk will be embarrassed that they were named, but I enumerate their efforts in hopes that others will duplicate them to help someone else in trouble.

The commentary by Dr. Jerry A. Patterson will inspire and encourage you. He was intimately involved in this horrific experience, and his observations will serve to inform you of just how much influence we can have on other individuals and that maintaining confidence in God is our utmost duty.

CHAPTER 1

SUMMER, 1961
THE ACCUSED

The freckle-faced boy wore a very short flat-top haircut, blue jeans, a short-sleeved pullover and Keds tennis shoes. He pushed up the kickstand on his bike with his right foot. After pushing off and swinging his leg over the bike seat, anyone seeing the look on his face would immediately recognize that he was one mighty proud young lad. He was enjoying the freedom that only a twelve-year-old can understand: freedom to ride almost anywhere he desired, freedom of being away from home and consistent parental oversight, freedom to visit friends, play baseball and hang out. Most of all, he enjoyed the freedom to still be a kid before the responsibilities of adulthood came careening into his life.

He was very proud of this bicycle his parents had given him as a present. It was fire-engine red and sported a bell on the handle bars that made a ringing sound by pressing a lever. Over the back fender were two baskets that were just the right size for those big, brown grocery bags that Bell's Food Market used to sack groceries. As he had done on many other days, he was going to the grocery store to pick up some items for his mom.

As the young boy mounted the bike and pushed off, it took him a moment to catch his balance as the front wheel swiveled left and right, and he struggled to get his feet onto the pedals. However, in just a second he had the bike moving forward, riding as smoothly as a grown-up teenager. Sometimes he rode his bike while sitting up straight. Other times he rode leaning way over the front handle bars while pretending he was a brave cowboy chasing after wild Indians. There were many times in the not too distant past when he rode his bike while dressed up as a cowboy: big cowboy hat, a red bandana around his neck, and two six-shooters strapped around his waist. Boy!! There was nothing like the smell and sound of exploding caps from his cap pistols. When he learned to steer his bike with one hand, no outlaw stood a chance against him. Later, when he had the skill to ride his bike without using either hand, he would use his BB rifle to shoot at every street sign on the block.

Now that he was twelve years old, dressing up like a cowboy was for little kids. He was currently into sports, particularly baseball. He would be entering junior high school come the fall school term. He had even started liking some girls and enjoyed talking with a couple of cute girls at church. He didn't understand why, but it was really cool to tell the guys about his "girlfriend."

He drove his bike to the neighborhood shopping area about three blocks from his home. The area featured a couple of strip centers, the largest including Bell's Food Market. The boy's mother sent him there two or three times a week to purchase a few items for their home. Across the street from the grocery store was a two-story apartment complex that housed several shops on the street level. Among the shops were a shoe store, a dress shop, a barber shop and a drug store that served the best sodas, ice cream and cherry Cokes in town. To one side of the grocery store stood a dry cleaners and a service station. On the other side of the grocery store, connected by a common wall, stood another business, a very simple, nondescript five and dime store.

On most trips he made to the grocery store, his mother would give him enough money to buy the items she wrote on a list, plus a little extra money to purchase something for himself. He would go into the store, walk the aisles picking up loaf bread, milk, bananas and peanut butter—whatever his mother listed. With the change, he would purchase a candy bar, or more often than not, he bought baseball cards he loved to collect. His mother was usually careful to not list too many items at one time because the baskets on his bike were only large enough to hold two bags. On the occasions when her list required three bags, he would place two of the bags in the baskets and hold the third bag while steering his bike with the other hand. To say the least, it was dangerous for anyone to be walking on the sidewalk in front of him when he was riding his bike this way.

When he first started making these trips a few years before, he would ride his bike straight to the grocery store, select his items, pay for them, and return straight home. This started when he was about eight years old. As the years went by, he became a very familiar figure riding his bike throughout the neighborhood. Traveling between home and the shopping area, between home and school, and visiting friends throughout the neighborhood, many people would recognize him and would wave or shout "hello" as he passed. Many times he would be stopped and neighbors would ask about his family or ask him to get something for them at the store, "while you're there." His favorite place to stop and visit while journeying through the neighborhood was Fire Station Number 3. Several of the firemen became his friends. He would stop to talk with them, play checkers, slide down the pole, play in the fire trucks and many times just sit in front of the fire hall to enjoy the weather. Many times he went to the grocery store for them and they would give him their change or a snack for making the trip.

As he grew older, his mother became accustomed to his occasional lateness in returning from the grocery store. Sometimes she would set a specific time for him to return. Other times she simply understood he would take advantage of his time out and would be visiting friends, the firemen or other neighbors. All in all, she trusted him to go to the grocery store, with occasional visits to the drug store or the barber shop, and return in a reasonable amount of time.

On this particular day, the young boy, after finishing his grocery shopping and placing the bags in the baskets on his bike, decided to go into the five and dime store to look around. He simply pushed his bike to the front of the store and parked it in front of the store window so that he could watch his bike and the bags that were in the baskets. He did not plan to stay in the five and dime store for a very long time. He had been in the store many times in the past to purchase sewing thread or small tools that his family needed. He was very familiar with the stock that the store carried and would stop in just to check the new toys that may have arrived. But mostly, he went in to check out that one constant in every red-blooded, all-American boy's life—the comic books.

This five and dime store maintained a large collection of comic books to sell. They were located on two spindle racks that sat on the left side, immediately near the front door. These racks were the kind that spun around and around. OH!! The selection: Superman, Super-Boy, Mickey Mouse, Goofy, Donald Duck, Archie, Combat, Sgt. Rock. There were so many to choose from and so many different varieties, from comedy to romance to war comics.

Over the years, the young boy had purchased numerous comic books. However, often times he would save his allowance by simply sitting down on the floor in the store and reading the comics right there. The store employees probably didn't like that very much and preferred that the comics be purchased and then taken home to be read. Because the young boy was a familiar sight in the store, they would indulge him as he sat on the floor next to the front door, leaning against the glass panel, engrossed in the latest episode of *Beetle Bailey.*

Being twelve years old meant that comic books no longer held the same attraction as they once did. He still enjoyed some of the more entertaining war comics, but he would not want any of his friends to catch him reading them. Reading comic books was no longer the trademark for someone trying to be cool and grown up. So, while he would scan the spindle racks when he walked into the store, just to see if anything new had come in, his main interest was the magazine rack against the wall, just behind the comic books. He discovered that there was a whole new world of grown up magazines that had gradually become more interesting than *Tom and Jerry* comic books.

He saw magazines that were geared for ladies, featuring fashions and hairdressing. These were definitely not his cup of tea. There were cooking and furniture magazines that didn't interest him either. He saw magazines about automobiles, auto racing and auto repairs, but these didn't spark a lot of interest. Then he discovered a series of magazines that made his eyes bug out: baseball magazines!

Man, this was great! The magazines told about all of the major league teams and displayed pictures of all the star players. They listed all of the team and player records, who was hitting the most home runs and who was striking out the most batters. They gave all of the box scores and every possible statistic. He saw pictures and read stories about many of his favorite ball players: Mickey Mantle, Roger Maris, Yogi Berra, Whitey Ford, Willie Mays, Joe Adcock, Hank Aaron, Warren Spahn and Eddie Mathews. He had also discovered that there were magazines that covered other sports like football and basketball. While he thought these other sports magazines were pretty cool, it was the baseball magazines that kept him coming back, time after time.

So on this particular day, when he entered the five and dime store, he bypassed the comic book spindles and stood directly in front of the magazine rack. After scanning the various magazine covers, he soon realized that he had already looked through all of the sports magazines available. The store was constantly changing the magazines and placing new issues out for purchase, but there just simply had not been enough time lapsed since he had last visited the five and dime store for them to receive new stock to display. He stood there gazing from shelf to shelf, hoping to locate a magazine that he could enjoy looking through before going home. After perusing all of the magazine covers that were displayed from just above his head to right below his chin, he decided to stoop down to look at the magazines displayed on the bottom shelves.

Lying flat on the bottom shelf were several newspapers. Above and just behind the newspapers were two shelves of magazines. The front shelf was filled with hunting and fishing magazines. There were also magazines for men's clothing and men's shoes. But just along the rear of the second shelf, in the furthest reaches of the magazine rack, were seven or eight magazines that carried some unusual titles. These were titles that the young boy had never seen nor recognized before then. One was called *Argosy*; another was entitled *Sir*. On another cover the word *Playboy* was displayed prominently. None of these titles raised any interest in the young boy; however, one title caught his eye, and he reached over to pull the magazine out. The title of the magazine was *Jaguar*.

Now the boy recognized the word, jaguar, and thought he knew that a jaguar was a very big and very fast cat. He also knew that the word represented the name of a very big and very fast car. Curious as to whether the magazine was about a feline or an automobile, he pulled the magazine out and looked at the cover. What he saw on the cover wasn't a cat or an automobile. Not even close. What he did see was a picture of a scantily-clad woman wearing an animal skin.

The young boy had never seen anything like this before in his life; neither in a cat nor in a car. His eyes opened wide and his mouth shaped an "O." Never before had he seen a picture of a female exposing so much skin. Though she was not completely uncovered, the look on her face and the stare in her eyes were a shock to the mind. He slowly and carefully opened the magazine and turned a few pages, revealing other photos similar to the one on the cover. After the initial shock, he actually felt like laughing—laughing at what he thought were pictures meant to be amusing and laughing at the thought that he was looking at something he shouldn't be looking at.

Suddenly he realized that he *shouldn't* be looking at those pictures. He didn't understand all of the thoughts and feelings that were being generated inside of his head, but he knew that somehow what he was doing was wrong. He shoved the magazine back into its place, probably damaging it to the point that it couldn't be sold. Nevertheless, that wasn't on his mind as he rushed out the door of the five and dime store. All he could think about was getting home where it was safe.

He grabbed his bike, kicked up the kickstand and pushed off with a hard shove, using all of his might. Jumping onto the bike as it was rapidly increasing in speed, he began to pedal furiously, rushing to get home. In his mind, he kept saying to himself, "I gotta get home. I gotta get home." Even as he pedaled as hard as he could, forcing his bike to go faster and faster, his mind would not let go of the images he had seen in the magazine. Though trying as hard as he knew how, even shaking his head vigorously trying to physically remove the photos from his memory, his mind's eye continued to wander back through those pictures, conjuring the images of those scantily-clad women to the forefront of his thinking.

Glad to get home, he rushed into the house carrying the groceries his mother had ordered. A part of him wanted to tell his mother about what he had seen, but he became so overwhelmed with shame that he simply could not say anything. Being a resilient youth, soon the episode retreated from memory, only to occasionally be brought back to mind throughout his lifetime when circumstances and events conspired. This event was the young man's first experience of being exposed to pornography. For the first time, he experienced how advertisement and media can introduce individuals to aspects of life they never knew existed, as well as lure them into trying "new things" when in reality they do not want to have anything to do with them.

As the young man grew into an adult and even into an older man, he encountered pornography all through his life. It would be difficult for any adult living in the United States in the 21st Century to avoid contact with pornography. It pervades our entertainment and advertisements. In many ways it has become a common aspect of our culture. As many, many adult men, he fought to keep pornography from influencing his life and spirituality. Pornography appears to bombard our male society on a consistent and daily basis. Every man must battle to maintain his integrity and not to allow this sinister and malicious evil called pornography to affect him or his family. Society and the law are not going to battle this for men. Each person is going to have to fight the battle himself.

Even with every effort being made to avoid pornography, its evil influence can still affect any person's life—even in a backhanded way. As you must understand, while this had been the first time this young man had been inadvertently affected by obscene materials, unfortunately it would not be the last time that pornography would rear its ugly and malicious head. The next time it would be in an attempt to nearly destroy this man's life. I know this for a fact because, you see, I was that young man.

CHAPTER 2

MONDAY, JANUARY 5, 2004-DAYTIME
THE ACCUSED

As I got dressed on this first Monday of the New Year, my mind was filled with anticipation, not only for the coming day but even for the upcoming year. During the previous year of 2003, my company, Southern Courthouse Ventures Legal Research Firm, had experienced its best year since its inception in 1990. My firm had grown to eleven staff and research associates, and with several new clients coming on board, I was planning to add more staff in the next few weeks. Currently, from our headquarters in the suburban Atlanta community of Conyers, my firm performed legal research in the Northern half of Georgia, through the central Macon area, and into the Savannah area. My business plan now called for me to add enough associates to perform property title research throughout the entire state of Georgia. In fact, after fourteen years of performing legal research in several area county courthouses, I was looking forward to becoming an "office manager." I felt I was finally going to be able to mange my business from my office while others performed the actual legwork of legal researching.

When I finished preparing to leave for the day, I asked my wife, Alison, what her plans were for the day. For the past nine years, she had not only been my marriage partner but my business partner as well. She had traveled to as many county courthouses as I had, performing the same type of legal research. She helped me build a business from a one man show to the point that we now had several employees, supporting several families. The Lord had so blessed our efforts that she was now able to remain at home and not physically travel from courthouse to court-house. Even though some physical ailments were beginning to affect her, she still chose to be involved and work in the office on a daily basis. I was thankful that our business was successful enough that she could work at a more leisurely pace, allowing her the time she needed to regain her strength and her health. After telling me she was going to work in the house for a while before going into the office, I kissed her on her cheek and stepped out my front door.

During the summer of 2002, I had a building erected next to my home that I converted into my office. Because of the restrictive covenants in the neighborhood where I live, I had it built so that from the street, it looked like a mother-in-law suite. The exterior materials and colors, green with a white trim, matched those of my house. Alison had made it look even more charming with the addition of a white picket fence with three gates placed in front of the Colonial red door. While the outside cosmetics and construction complemented our house, the inside was all business. For it was from the inside of "the cottage," as we named it, that all of the functions of my legal research firm were handled.

The greatest majority of my business is handled by fax, e-mail, or courier service. My clients are companies situated all across the United States. I don't have walk-in customers, only employees and delivery people visit "the cottage." However, when Alison and I had the building erected, we decided to make it as charming and comfortable as possible. When you walk into the front door, you enter into a huge room with an open ceiling all the way up to the roofline. In the center of the room is a dividing wall with passages both to the left and right gaining access to the rear of the office. A huge wooden beam across the center supports the wall with some open space above the top of the wall to the roof. Behind the wall at the rear of the room is a restroom and a kitchen area with a sink, microwave and refrigerator. One of the striking features of the room noticed immediately upon entering is a work of art painted directly on the center wall depicting a Colonial scene around the Williamsburg, Virginia courthouse. Above the painting hangs a tri-corn hat from the American Revolutionary era. Throughout the office are Colonial

flower vases and candleholders with many pen draw-
ings of old Georgia courthouses.

Despite the Colonial atmosphere and charm, it's
easy to tell that this is a workplace. The office area is
filled with workstations, computers, telephones, fax
machines, scanners and way too many file cabinets.
My four office staff members are usually talking
on the telephones, standing at the fax machines,
pounding away on the computer keyboards, or doing
all three things at once! Most of the legal research
work my office performs involves property and
titles. The office staff is consistently communicating
with our clients and with the researchers in the courthouses. My office staff have proven their loyalty on
many occasions when they've either come in early,
before the telephones start ringing at 9:00 A.M., or
stayed over later than 5:00 P.M. to catch up on files
or research orders. Alison and I both have thanked
God for such devoted and hard-working employees.

It is such a convenient walk for me from my front
door to the door of my office. It's only a few steps
from my place of rest and relaxation into the professional world of business. I went into my office this
Monday morning to review the requests for research
and to plan my itinerary. As usual, I prepared myself
to be visiting three to four of the area courthouses in
order to fill the search requests from our clients. While
scanning the faxes requesting property research and
planning the route for the day, Sean Peacock came in
with a "morning, Chief." I had brought Sean onto my
staff back in October of 2003, and he had completed
his in-house training for legal research the previous

week. He had accompanied me to two or three of the area courthouses the week after Christmas, but this was to be his first full week of traveling with me. This was to be the beginning of his in-courthouse legal research training. He was to work with me for several weeks before I would designate him several county courthouses in which he would perform legal research on his own.

Sean is an enthusiastic young man and was excited about finally being able to go into a courthouse and perform an actual search. He had spent several weeks in the office with my staff bombarding him with vocabulary and research methods. He was glad to no longer be confined in a small area with four women. Additionally, he was anticipating making research commissions, certainly much better pay than his modest training salary. Plus, he had an additional motivation to begin performing legal researches on his own: he and his wife, Carla, were expecting their first child in April (Louis Robert Peacock was born April 20, 2004).

I had retained fifteen out of ninety counties as my own personal research area, while maintaining oversight on the work of the other researchers. I thoroughly enjoyed legal research, particularly research involving title chains and property. To me it was like putting a puzzle together. You gathered and put all of the pieces together and presented the client a complete picture of the property. I had started my company in 1990, and after fourteen years, it appeared that I was finally going to wind down and go into a different direction with my vocation.

That's the reason I was excited about Sean. He was going to be taking over the heart of my company, my own personal research area. I had performed searches for my clients within this area since I had started up my company. I knew many of the courthouse personnel in each county, as well as many of the other title researchers and attorneys who worked in those courthouses. Throughout the years as my company grew, I had always retained this area as my own for two reasons. One, I knew the people in these courthouses well, from the security guards and the maintenance crew to the clerks and judges. Secondly, I completely enjoyed the scenic area that fills the central part of Georgia, from the Southern Atlanta suburbs to metropolitan Macon. While it was extremely difficult to imagine that I would not be visiting these courthouses very much longer, I was excited about the potential growth my company would enjoy when I would finally have the time to concentrate on training new researchers and developing new clients.

As Sean and I got into my 2003 Ford Taurus SEL, I told him that I was planning to turn my area over to him completely by the end of January. Because of ongoing negotiations and bids for my company to provide legal research in all 159 Georgia counties, I explained to him that I wanted him to learn to handle the workload in this area so that during the month of February, I could intensely train three new researchers in the South Georgia region. With these new researchers, my legal research firm would be able to advertise that it could provide service throughout the entire state of Georgia. After February, I planned to work with each of my researchers for a week at a time until summer arrived. After that, I hoped to visit clients in Ohio and California to negotiate new and expanded contracts. Sean's enthusiasm and my plans inspired our conversation as we drove to a couple of county courthouses, working our way toward Macon, GA.

The Bibb County Courthouse located in Macon is a grand old building, giving that solid look that befits law and justice. At a little after 1:00 P.M. we entered the main lobby, passed through security and walked directly to the county tax assessor's office. After securing the information we needed, we walked to the deed records area maintained by the Clerk of the Superior Court. The deed record room is a huge area consisting of numerous shelves of books, computer stations and tall legal tables on which to work. Approximately twenty other researchers were already there working on their various projects. Several of them spoke to me and I introduced them to Sean. A couple of the researchers told us that if at any time in the future Sean needed any assistance or help that they would be glad to help him. I guess they figured that after I turned the area over to him and became semi-retired that I would not be of much help to him! I told them that I wasn't planning to go anywhere in any big hurry and that they would have to put up with me aggravating them for a while longer.

At approximately 2:45 P.M., Alison beeped over on my cell phone. I always kept my phone speaker set "on" so I could hear if either she or my office staff called, but as soon as I heard her say "Jim," I pushed the speaker button to "off" and clicked over to her with "hi there."

"Are you where you can talk to me?" she asked.

From the tone of her voice I felt like she had something serious on her mind—how serious I could have never guessed.

I walked over to a quiet corner of the record room and said, "Sure. My phone speaker is off. What do you need?"

"Jim," she said, "the GBI (Georgia Bureau of Investigation) is here with several deputies from the Rockdale County Sheriff's Department. They have a search warrant to get all of our computers, both from the house and the office. The warrant says that they are searching for child pornography on our computers."

THE WIFE

At first, hearing the doorbell ring and then looking out through the window in the front door to see who was on my porch, I thought the men and women assembled there must be from a church. I opened the door thinking I might be meeting Mormons or Jehovah's Witnesses, but rather, I was met with some very serious expressions upon their faces. These people weren't here for witnessing. No, they were here on a mission—a mission to close in on a vile ring of evil people! I told them to come on in so that we could get started with what they needed to do.

Once inside, this group of law enforcement seemed to be angrier than they had been outside my door. One gentleman even said something to the effect that I wasn't taking this serious and asked me if I knew how serious it was, as if I were a complete idiot. I told him that I did realize it was serious.

I was quite glad to have a reason to call Jim and let him know we had some "visitors." This gave me a chance to ask him if these people, who were filling up our house, would have any legitimate reason for being here. I also had the chance to ask him, in my sweetest voice possible, when he would be home. It's somewhat difficult to smile while gritting your teeth.

THE ACCUSED

I don't know if I can describe totally what I felt at that moment, but I think that my mind literally froze for several seconds. My mind went blank as I tried to absorb what Alison was saying. It was so unexpected, completely out of the blue. It's possible that my face blanched as my mind reeled from a hundred different thoughts and emotions. Why? What brought this on? What's going on? What am I suppose to do? Never in a million years could I conceive of something like this happening to me! I must not have been able to say anything at that moment for then Alison went on...

"They're asking Debbie and the other girls a lot of questions, and they want to know when you are coming back."

"Okay, Alison," I said. "Just let them look at whatever and wherever they want. It will take me at least an hour and a half to drive back to Conyers from here. I'll get there as soon as I can. Are you okay?"

"It's been a little crazy here. They've been all over the house, and they've taken all of the computers out of here and out of the office. We're going to have problems running our business without the computers. They wouldn't even let Debbie shut the computers down and save our business records."

"I'm so sorry this is happening," I told her. "It's going to be okay. I'll be back there as soon as I can."

Even though I had said everything would be okay, I definitely had no assurance of that. I was totally and shockingly stunned. As I clicked my cell phone off, I felt like a zombie. Even though I began to walk back into the main area of the deed record room, I felt like I was almost watching my legs and arms move while standing outside of my body. I just could not believe that this was happening to ME!! Here I was, fifty-four years old, and outside of traffic violations, I had never been in any kind of trouble, especially with the law. I haven't been a gangster. I haven't been a criminal. Yet this has to be real. It's not a movie. It's not a show. I'm not reading a book. This is really happening. And as the reality began to sink in, my mind began crying out, "Oh, God! What am I going to do?!"

THE OFFICE MANAGER

What does one do when "the authorities" show up at the door? To me, on that cold and rainy January day, it meant putting on company manners. You know, setting work aside and being as polite, cheerful and helpful as possible. God's children know how to experience fearful situations without being afraid. It's similar to being in a city of refuge, a place of safety in time of danger. How does one gain entrance to such a city? It takes determination and faith—determination to maintain integrity and faith that God will reward such action by supplying a safety net. As the Lord told Satan regarding Job, because Job had held fast to his integrity, "...you must save his life."

Little did I know, in the beginning, how long things would last and how very difficult things would become.

THE ACCUSED

Sean had continued to work on one of our property research projects and came over toward me to ask some questions about some of the information he had found. I mentally shook my head, trying to overcome the shock I was feeling and concentrate on going one step at a time. I said to myself, "Okay, let's see how quickly we can finish up here and head back to Rockdale County, where my home lays waiting in shock and turmoil." I answered Sean's questions then I told him...

"Let's see if we can finish this work up in about fifteen minutes, and then we'll head on out." Sean knew we were expected to go to another county courthouse on the way back to the office so he did not think my statement was unusual. Actually, I was dreading the trip back. I think subconsciously I was delaying the return as long as possible. I just needed time to think this whole nightmare through.

THE WIFE

I told the law officers to look anywhere they wanted, to make themselves at home. They seemed quite baffled by my behavior. In the meantime, they wanted to open a locked trunk in Jim's study. I told them I was not sure where the keys were. I put in another call to Jim.

THE ACCUSED

Just then Alison beeped me again with "Jim." I walked back to my quiet corner, switching my speaker to "off" and answered her, "Yes?"

"The GBI are still here and the deputies too. They want to know where the key to the trunk in your library is."

Alison and I had converted one of our upstairs bedrooms into the "library." One whole wall and one half of another wall are filled with bookshelves that almost reach the ceiling. I have my father's desk and chair in the library where I normally sit and write. Also, there are two Queen Anne cushioned library chairs with a small library table sitting between them. I enjoy sitting in those chairs to read, and they make for a comfortable setting when friends visit. Behind my desk is a work station that holds my computer. In front of my desk sits a one hundred and fifty year old travel trunk that had belonged to my great-great-great-grand uncle, William Gray. It was a square box with two snap locks along the front and a big key lock in the center front panel. The investigators were inspecting every nook and cranny in my office for some kind of evidence and had determined that they wanted to see what was inside of that locked trunk.

I replied, "I think the key is either in the gun rack over the trunk or is in the basket sitting on my night stand."

"Okay, Jim, hold on a second."

After a moment, I asked, "Did you tell them there's nothing in that old trunk but sheets and blankets and pillow cases?"

"Yes, but they said they still wanted to look in there anyway. Okay, here's the key. Hold on a second."

THE WIFE

Returning to Jim's study, I told one of the men standing to go ahead and break the lock on the trunk if he felt that was necessary. I told them that I was pretty sure the only contents were sheets and blankets. For the first time this man, who had earlier acted impatient with me, seemed to realize I was only trying to help him and was not a candidate for America's

Most Wanted. Especially after the key was located and the trunk contents proved to be exactly as I told him—sheets and blankets, which were stored in the trunk for periodic and seasonal changes of linens.

THE ACCUSED

I don't know if I appeared nervous, disturbed or distraught to anyone who may have noticed me standing there, but I knew I was becoming a nervous wreck. Surprisingly, it was during this time that I actually thought about my heart. Two years before, upon receiving the news that my father had suffered a heart attack, I had suffered a minor heart attack myself. Over the next two weeks, after my father passed away and we had conducted his funeral services, I suffered three more heart seizures. This eventually led to quadruple by—pass surgery in January 2002. Previous to that, I had an angioplasty procedure in March of 1997 and a stint procedure in December of 1998. I could tell my stress level was rising rapidly because of the news from Alison, but my heart didn't hurt and my chest remained painless. I wondered how in the world I *wasn't* hurting!

"Jim?" Alison asked.

"Yes?" I softly replied.

"The deputies say they are satisfied. One of them commented that I was right and that there wasn't anything in that old trunk but sheets and blankets. When are you coming back?"

I glanced at the clock on the deed room wall, and it read almost 3:00 P.M. I beeped over and said, "It will be at least 4:30 before I can get back, but I'll be there as soon as possible. Are you still doing okay?"

Alison's voice had not sounded shaky or nervous at all. In fact, I was very proud as to how she was apparently handling this total disruption to her life. She was talking in a very matter-of-fact manner. She is a very strong person in a time of crisis or stress. She can only reveal how stressed she really is in a private setting.

"Yes, I'm still okay," she replied. "The GBI agents and the deputies have been nice and courteous. I've answered all of their questions to the best I know how and they've told me that they appreciate my cooperation. I think they're leaving now. I'll talk to you later."

"Okay, hon. Bye."

THE WIFE

What I did next is the most important part of my story. I called my pastor, Dr. Jerry Patterson. The bottom line is, if I hadn't had him, there could have been a very different ending to my part in this occurrence. You cannot put any dollar amount on how much your pastor can help you in a time like this. I had to do some serious thinking and two different scenarios were dominant in my mind. Dr. Patterson's help was essential in helping me determine what to do.

First, I thought about Jim's children and about my children. I definitely wanted our marriage to be for a lifetime, not just for us but for them also. I had never really understood what "no man is an island" meant until I heard Dr. Patterson teach that "whatever you do affects others." This lesson now had a practical application to my life. It wasn't just about me—there were children involved! I wanted to stay married! I loved Jim! I wanted our children to be able to count on us.

The second scenario involved my thoughts about our grandchildren. I couldn't stand by Jim *if* he was guilty of any kind of crime. That would send a bad message all the way around.

THE DOCTOR

I was out of town in a meeting when my wife called and gave me a message to call Alison Reynolds as soon as possible. She provided little information except to tell me that the Rockdale County Sheriff's Department, along with the Georgia Bureau of Investigation, were at Jim and Alison's office and home in the process of taking all of their computers into custody. I asked my wife how Alison sounded on the telephone, and she replied that she seemed to be in control but confused as to why this was happening. My wife suggested I call her as soon as possible.

I have known Jim and his family all of my life. I grew up in a church where he had relatives and he and his family visited our church on many occasions. I had also seen them at various District church functions. In addition, Jim and I had attended the same college and I was later his pastor for about ten tears in Athens, Georgia. It was during this time that we became very close friends. Jim was bright, creative and very hard working and I enjoyed our relationship. I am also Jim's pastor in Conyers, Georgia and have been for over twenty years.

I had not known Alison Reynolds for as long. I met her when she began attending our church in 1993, some thirteen years ago. I worked with her at the church office and knew her to be intelligent, energetic, creative and gentle. I enjoyed the time we worked together in the office. Later, she became involved in the organizing of a Boy Scouts of America program in our church. She did an absolutely excellent job in this area as well. Jim and Alison later married, and I was happy for the both of them and have continued to enjoy a close relationship with them as a couple. They are devoted members of Faith Tabernacle Church and have been loyal to me through the years. Most recently, when I went through a personal crisis in the church, they were loyal and supportive for which I will always be deeply grateful.

When I returned Alison's call, she sounded calm, serious and still a little confused as to exactly what was going on with the Sheriff's Department and the GBI. She had a lot of questions about the present and the future for both her and Jim. I set up an appointment with her for the next day.

THE ACCUSED

Somehow, with my head reeling in a thousand different directions, Sean and I finished the research projects we had and left the Bibb County Courthouse around 3:15 P.M. As we started down the courthouse steps, I tossed Sean my car keys and said, "You can drive."

He asked, "Are we still going to stop at the Monroe County Courthouse?"

I told him, "No. We've got to head straight back to the office. I'll tell you why in the car."

The drive from Bibb County back to Rockdale County usually takes one hour and fifteen minutes. It took longer that day because of a heavy rain storm and unusually slow traffic. But I can't say that I was in any hurry. If there could have been some way to avoid having to go back home, I would have probably taken it. I just felt like I was in a serious situation that was going to be difficult to handle. Not fully understanding all of the dynamics involved in having a search warrant served, along with the trauma my wife and office staff had been through, made the situation very unnerving. I felt sure that a mistake had been made and that I could not be guilty of whatever the GBI was accusing me. I was definitely entering into an arena that I was totally unprepared to enter. I was at a loss as to how to approach this nerve-wrecking situation. It was difficult for me to even get a straight line of thought going in my head. My mind was constantly reeling from one thought to another, and it was becoming very difficult to gain a true focus. In the past, I had found that talking aloud about a problem allowed me the time and opportunity to develop a sensible and logical plan. I was reluctant to involve Sean in the situation by discussing it with him, but I realized that when we returned to the office he would learn of the predicament anyhow. I decided to reveal what had happened and at the same time see if a discussion would open up my mind and help me to focus on what my next step should be.

Sean had already driven us out of downtown Macon and had climbed the ramp onto I-75 North when I began to tell him of the day's occurrences. I explained to him about Alison's calls and how the Rockdale County Sheriff's Department had seized all five of my business and personal computers. When he asked what I thought was going on, I told him that over the past two years our computers had suffered from spam, pop-ups and several computer viruses. I had paid some computer technicians to install firewalls and spam blockers, but I began to think it was a losing battle. We continued to have pop-ups and viruses that advertised everything from insurance, mortgage rates and travel to gambling and pornography—even child pornography. It appeared to me that the investigation was the result of an accusation that I was somehow harboring child pornography.

At that moment I was not totally aware of the nature of the charges that caused the search warrant. My mind was soaring into vast arenas of speculation as I pondered the situation. I had seen the pop-ups and advertisements for pornography from time to time, even for child pornography. I had, through morbid curiosity, looked at the advertisements, but I had never, in any way, shape, manner or form, deliberately or accidentally downloaded a file, copied an image or attempted to save a picture of any description. I was not very computer literate. My knowledge and ability on a computer was very limited. I did not know how to save files or download pictures. I had never needed that kind of knowledge, and I just never attempted to seek it. However, it appeared that law enforcement officials had determined that I was concealing images and pictures of child pornography with criminal intent.

I told Sean that Alison had advised me that the Sheriff Deputies had requested that I come to their offices when I got back into town to answer a few of their questions. Sean immediately stated that the best thing I could do was have an attorney go with me. I admit that my mind and emotions were so rattled and unsteady that I had not even thought of that. I listed in my mind several attorneys that I knew who would be more than capable of assisting me, but the one that jumped into my mind as being the most competent and who I thought knew me the best was Garland "Gary" Moore. Gary and his wife, Irene, had lived directly across the street from me for more than ten years.

I was still so shook up that I asked Sean to get Gary's office telephone number for me. As Sean continued to drive up rain-slicked I-75, I called Gary's office in Conyers. I begin to think back on how Gary Moore and his family had been the first family that Alison and I met when we moved into the neighborhood in 1994. Many times, Gary and I had stood in our yards at the end of our cul-de-sac or in the street between our homes and discussed the neighborhood and current events. Gary had run for public office and I was proud to have supported him and even contributed financially to his campaign. Not only was Gary a successful attorney, but he also served Rockdale County as a Magistrate Judge. He and his wife continued to be active politically and socially in the area.

Gary answered in his slow and deliberate manner of speaking I immediately recognized, "Garland Moore speaking."

"Hi Gary, this is Jim Reynolds. I believe I am in need of your professional services. Do you have a minute to talk with me?"

"Sure, Jim. What can I do for you?"

I explained to Gary what had occurred at my home earlier that afternoon. He said that his wife had already told him about seeing the GBI vans and Sheriff Department vehicles in the neighborhood. He asked me a few questions, but I was only able to answer, "I don't know." He told me he would leave his office in a little while and would meet me at my house around five o'clock. As Sean and I pulled in front of my house, Gary drove up behind us and pulled into his driveway.

As I got out of my car, I decided to check on my office staff before going into my house. I was concerned for Alison, but I knew the office staff would be leaving momentarily and that I would probably be talking with Alison for a long time that evening. I wanted to somehow assure my office staff that everything would be all right, even though I didn't actually feel all that confident.

THE ASSOCIATE

I was with Jim the day the GBI raid took place on his house and office. My initial reaction was one of disbelief. I didn't think that they had the right house or the right man (A thought that was later found to be totally true.) This was a man who had gone out of his way to help me and my family when our backs were against the wall. A man who took his time, money and energy to teach me a skill and profession that I could make a living using. And he did this without a guarantee that it would even pay off in the long run, only my word that I would do my best for him.

I watched as his countenance just fell. Jim Reynolds is probably one of the most giving men that I have ever met. And now, he was being accused of a grossly selfish crime, a crime that just didn't fit "the profile" of the man that I knew.

THE ACCUSED

I walked in the chilling rain past my house toward "the cottage." I do not remember for sure, but I think all four of my staff was still there. I was immediately inundated with their reactions to the day's events. They told me about the GBI agents removing the computers without giving them a chance to close their work schedules and search reports. They questioned me as to how we were going to be able to operate the company without the computers. We talked for a few minutes about different strategies to initiate for the rest of the week. I told them that I thought the computers were only going to be gone temporarily and that, if necessary, I would purchase new ones. The main system we would miss the most was the unique program they utilized to track search requests and our bookkeeping.

I assured them that I would let them know about everything that was going on as it happened. I expressed my sincere appreciation for the way they had handled the unfortunate incident and they in turn told me that they were behind me, loved me and believed in me. I apologized to them for the intrusion into their lives and that all of it was my responsibility. This was the first in a long list of apologies that I would make in the coming weeks.

CHAPTER 3

MONDAY, JANUARY 5, 2004-EVENING THE ACCUSED

As the sun began its quickening descent behind the still lowering and dark rain clouds, I left my office and began the short walk back to my front door and to Alison. I knew she had been through a horrible and traumatic experience-one she would have never anticipated. To have Deputy Sheriffs and GBI Investigators pull in front of her home in their cars and vans, enter and serve a warrant to search through her home for evidence of child pornography, proceed to remove all of the computers in the house and in the office had to be more than disheartening and disruptive. After going through the house and opening every door, every drawer and looking behind every picture, she had to feel devastated. I didn't exactly know what to expect when I saw her.

I would not have been surprised to find a very angry and upset woman. I knew she would be, at least, very worried and very uncertain about what the coming days would hold. However, what I found was a woman who, while she was very concerned about the situation, was a very strong and forthright wife and basically said, "We're going to work this out, and we're going to work it out together." When I entered the house, Alison met me in the living room.

"Are you all right?" I asked.

"Yes. I'm okay. I think I'm still recovering from the shock," she replied.

"I'm so sorry for all of this. I feel so bad that you had to go through what you did today. I would not have had you go through anything like this for the entire world."

Little did I realize that she wasn't the only one who was going to have "to be put through this."

I asked her to tell me what happened. In a nutshell, she said that she had been taken completely by surprise when a knock was made at the front door. She looked out the side window, saw what she recognized as law enforcement personnel, and she immediately opened the door. She was confronted by deputies from the Rockdale County Sheriffs Department and investigators from the Georgia Bureau of Investigation. One of them handed her a piece of paper and said that they were there to seize our computers and to look for other evidence of child pornography. She said that several stern-looking male and female officers came into the house searching throughout every room. She saw other officers outside taking pictures. Soon my office staff came in and advised that the computers in the office were also being taken out. Throughout the entire time that the officers were there, Alison and the other ladies from my office answered every question with respect and courtesy. Alison even went so far as to ask the officers if there was anything else she could do for them. She told them that she wanted to assist them in any way that she could. I learned later that evening from one of the female officers who searched my home that she and the other officers commented on "how nice" and "fully cooperative" everyone was at my home and office. Also, Alison said she had called our pastor, Dr. Jerry Patterson, and informed him of the incident.

Just then, Gary Moore knocked on the front door, and I opened the door for him. Gary can be a very soft-spoken individual. In fact, there are times that he speaks so softly that I have to ask him to repeat what he said. Of course, that may have a lot to do with the fact that the older I get, the harder my hearing becomes. In every situation I've seen Gary, he is always the same as I saw him right then. His presence is one of professionalism, confidence and assurance. He knows what he is doing. He came right in, shook our hands, and said, "Okay, what's going on?"

I gave him the copy of the search warrant as Alison briefly told him of the events that day. As she was talking, Gary read the search warrant wherein it was declared that the warrant was being served because of alleged violations of Volume 16, Book 12, Article 100, Section B and Paragraph 5 which states: "It is unlawful for any person knowingly to create, reproduce, publish, promote, sell, distribute, give, exhibit, or possess with intent to sell or distribute any visual medium which depicts a minor or a portion of a minor's body engaged in any sexually explicit conduct."

Alison then excused herself while I explained to Gary that the only child pornography that I had seen was from the pop-ups, spam and advertisements that came over our computers unsolicited. He asked if I knew any reason this would have caused a search warrant to be issued, and I told him that I didn't know of any reason. I told him that I had not purchased any child pornography; I had not used any credit cards to purchase pornography. I had not requested pictures by e-mail, nor had I been in any chat rooms trying to obtain porn. I had not downloaded or copied any pictures at all, much less child pornography. I expressed my surprise and shock and said that I had absolutely no other idea what had caused the investigation. Having told him earlier on the telephone that the Sheriffs Department had requested that I come down to their office and answer a few questions, he asked me if I was prepared to go. I answered that I guessed I was as ready as I would ever be. He told me to tell Alison that I would be back soon.

I called Alison downstairs and told her that I was going with Gary to the Sheriffs Department, just as they requested. She gave me a quick hug and said that she would wait up for me. Gary and I then walked out, crossed the street and got into his automobile. The Sheriffs Department and County Jail was about a twenty minute drive.

As Gary drove, he asked me a few more questions. At this writing, I cannot recall the questions, but I probably answered with "I don't know" the majority of the time. I do recall being somewhat nervous and even felt a quiver and shaking in my stomach. I had never been in this kind of situation before in my life, and I was more than concerned; I was scared. Not afraid of my guilt or innocence, but afraid of the unknown. My mind was racing, "What's going to happen? What are they going to ask? How will they ask their questions? Are they going to bombard me with hundreds of questions? Will it be detectives or deputies or the Sheriff? Will they tag-team me? Will they lock me up for questioning? Are there things going on that I don't know?" Scores of questions were going through my mind, but I was having difficulty articulating them to Gary.

Gary told me, as we got closer to the Sheriffs Department, that when we went in, I was not to answer any questions or to say anything unless he said so. He told me that the first thing he was going to determine was if they had an arrest warrant for me.

Arrest? ARREST?!? You've got to be kidding me. Arrest? That thought had not even entered into my mind. Arrested? Fingerprinted, jailhouse picture, orange jumpsuit kind of arrest? I have to admit that while I can have a vivid imagination, I just could not conjure up that kind of picture with me in it.

Gary continued to say that if they had issued an arrest warrant, I was not to say a word and not to answer any question whatsoever unless he was present. He also said that as soon as they completed the arrest, he would immediately go before a judge to have a bond set. He said he would do everything in his power to make sure that I was not held but for a minimum amount of time and certainly not overnight. It was comforting to know that Gary had a plan to keep me from having to stay any length of time in jail; however, the very thought of being arrested and incarcerated was difficult and incomprehensible. In fifty-four years, I had not ever been arrested, much less placed in a jail cell. The thoughts of that were unimaginable.

By the time we arrived at the parking lot outside of the Sheriffs Department, my apprehension must have become quite apparent. Having known about my previous bouts with heart trouble, Gary asked me, "You're not going to crash on me, are you?"

Not understanding what he meant, I replied, "Excuse me?"

"I heard you breathe a little heavy, and I was afraid that you might start having a heart attack on me or something."

I don't think breathing hard is even the beginning of how I feel, I thought. I told him I wasn't having any heart problems but that I was feeling very uncomfortable and nervous. He told me to just try and relax and that he would handle the interview and determine just exactly where we stood.

We entered the front door of the Rockdale County Sheriffs Department located at 911 Chambers Drive, Conyers. We walked into a waiting area with receptionists sitting behind glass windows. Gary walked up to one window and announced our presence. A few minutes later, Captain Warren S. Summers opened the door to the inner offices and introduced himself. It appeared from his facial expression that he had not expected me to appear with an attorney. He shook our hands, gave us his name, and then led us through a dimly lit office area, heavily populated with desks and chairs. He directed us into a small side room described by a sign on the door that said, "Interview Room 1." It was a very non-descript narrow room with three chairs and a desk.

After sitting, Gary asked Captain Summers, "Do you have an arrest warrant for Mr. Reynolds?" My heart felt like it was stuck in my throat until Captain Summers said, "No." Mentally, I gave the biggest sigh of relief imaginable. Captain Summers proceeded to explain what had happened leading up to their investigation and the service of the search warrant.

During November 2003, an Internet Watch Group discovered a new child pornography website. They proceeded to report this new site to the Georgia Bureau of Investigation. The GBI obtained from the web host company, located in Chicago, Illinois, a copy of the application and contract to open the website. The application indicated that the owner of the new child pornography website was James Curtis Reynolds—me! The GBI then contacted the Rockdale County Sheriffs Department, and in cooperation together, they were able to obtain a search warrant from Superior Court Judge David Irwin.

I admit I was stunned. I was in total shock at these allegations. I felt like I was in the middle of a nightmare, and I just wanted someone to please wake me up. I began to feel a little better for one very good reason—I had never been involved with the creation, opening or establishment of any kind of website, legal or illegal. I didn't even know how to begin to open a website much less operate one. The only problem that I saw at that time was being able to prove to the investigators that their allegations were totally in error.

Captain Summers reached for an envelope that he had brought in with him and removed a couple of pieces of paper. He explained that the top page was a copy of the cover page for the website in question. I was only given about a two second glance at the page before he turned and handed it to Gary. What I remember seeing was a page that appeared to have come from a pop-up, but I am not certain. It featured a collage of photographs of what appeared to be children involved in various sexual activities and poses. My view was so limited that I was unable to make a definitive determination. My first instinct was that it was possible that I may have seen something similar during some pop-up or spam invasion, but I had certainly not seen that page within the context presented. I do know that brief glimpse left me feeling the same as when I had viewed pop-ups on previous occasions: ill, nauseated, angry, saddened, shocked, dismayed and by that time, emotionally drained.

After handing the first page to Gary, Captain Summers gave me a brief glimpse of the second page. He stated that this was a photocopy of the application made to open the website. Again, I was only afforded a few seconds to scan the page when

Captain Summers turned and gave this page to Gary. So far, the only words I had spoken were in greeting when we first met Captain Summers. After seeing the second page of "evidence" that they were using to support their allegations, I could not restrain myself any longer. I sat forward and said, "While the information there appears to be accurate as far as my name, address and social security number, this is not an e-mail address that I have used. I have never used yahoo.com."

One of the first things that I noticed after seeing that my name, address and social security number had been listed correctly on the application was a glaring inaccurate e-mail address. What had been written into a space asking for an e-mail contact was written something like, "JAMESCURTISREYNOLDS12@ YAHOO.COM." The only e-mail address I had ever had and maintained for several years was jimreyscv@ aol.com. A friend, George Chandler, had helped me set up an AOL account and had advised me that I should not use the full spelling of any part of my name as a safety precaution and better security. He suggested that I use something close to the spelling of my name so that people who received any e-mails could recognize that it was me sending them the e-mail. Upon seeing what had been written as the e-mail contact address, I felt I had an important and valid point to show that I had not been involved in establishing a child porn website.

After I made my statement, Captain Summers replied, "Anyone can open another e-mail address, particularly with yahoo, because it doesn't cost anything with them." It felt like he was trying to shoot my "valid" point right out of the water.

Gary shook his head at me, which I understood to mean, "Stop talking." I sat back, wondering how in the world this had happened. The information on the application for the website was very accurate— too accurate to say the least. I believe this is the first inkling I had that someone had taken my identity and used it to open a child porn website. Now I was being accused of owning and operating it.

Captain Summers excused himself and left us alone. Gary asked, "What did you see?"

I said, "Besides the e-mail address being wrong, my middle name, Curtis, was listed. I infrequently use my middle name, particularly in business or legal matters. I never use my middle name on credit cards. I only use my middle initial, 'C'."

I wasn't too sure about the social security number or the credit card number, but later I found out that they were both accurate.

The office door opened, Captain Summers entered and immediately stated that he and the other detectives were interested in reviewing my credit card records and bank statements, in particular the credit card listed on the website application. He said that they had retrieved a lot of my records that day but were unable to locate any information concerning that particular credit card. Gary and I stood up, and he told Captain Summers that we would return the next morning with as much pertinent information as we could. Captain Summers asked if I could provide the information for that credit card, and I told him that I thought I would be able to and that I would be glad to do it. Captain Summers then escorted us back through the office to the lobby and said, "Good night." Throughout the interview, Captain Summers had spoken to me with respect and had always referred to me as, "Mr. Reynolds." I appreciated his demeanor toward me.

As we walked out the front door, I didn't think anyone could imagine how relieved I felt to be walking out of that place. Little could I imagine that I would feel even greater relief when I walked out of that place sometime afterward.

As we got in the car and drove away, Gary asked me again about what I saw on the application that I felt was in error. I reviewed what I had said earlier and expressed the hope that we could review it again in detail. He said that would probably happen. He then asked how much financial information I could provide him by tomorrow morning. I thought I could immediately put my hands on at least a year's worth of credit card and bank account statements. He then asked if I thought I could gather two years worth. I told him that was possible. He said that if we provided more information than they were asking for, it would show that we were cooperating with them fully. When we arrived at Gary's house and I exited his vehicle, he told me to bring all of the financial information that I gathered to his office at nine o'clock the next morning. I told him I would, shook his hand and walked across the street to my home.

Inside, I found Alison waiting patiently. Despite the emotional uproar the events of the day had caused her, she appeared outwardly calm as we sat down and I reviewed for her what had occurred at the Sheriffs Department. She quickly surmised, "But you don't even know how to create a website of any description much less an illegal one."

I told her she was right about that but that now I had to gather together a lot of our financial information in order to counteract the website application that Captain Summers had shown me. I told her that I was going to stay up for a while longer to look for the paperwork because I had to take it by Gary's office before taking them to the Sheriffs Department. She offered to help me, but I encouraged her to go on to bed and rest. I felt the stress of the day would aggravate her back, shoulder and neck pain that she suffered on an almost daily basis. Plus, I felt totally responsible for all that had happened that day and for the whole situation. I felt like I should have been on guard and prevented anything like that from happening. I felt anger that my wife and employees had suffered such embarrassment through this uncomfortable situation. I didn't think it necessary for anyone else to have to suffer from these events. Nor should anyone have to do any work to help extricate me from these trying circumstances. I felt it necessary for me to work on my own, by myself. I felt so ashamed that I really didn't want to ask anyone else to help me.

First, I went out to my office area and quickly accumulated all of my bank and credit card statements for 2003. I took all of those up to my library and then went to the garage and retrieved the storage boxes that held my 2002 financial records. I took these to my library and began sorting the paperwork. After about a half hour, Alison came into the library and said she couldn't sleep and that she would really like to help. We worked together for about an hour, sorting the financial data into workable stacks.

When we finished, it was about 10:30 P.M.. Alison went back to bed, but I continued to sit at my desk, reviewing the records lying in front of me. In a few minutes, I made a remarkable discovery. I found that the most current credit card statements received during the month of December 2003 were not in any of my stacks. I immediately opened the top right drawer of my desk and removed my bookkeeping record book. This is a book in which I record the income from my business, plus I record all of the expenses. I knew it was an old fashioned method and that most businesses let their computers keep their books, however, I was very comfortable keeping my records by hand. I kept receipts from paid bills and invoices clipped to the book so that I would remember which payments to record. After recording the payments, the invoices and receipts were stored in a file cabinet located in my office until income tax time.

When I opened my bookkeeping record book, I located the receipts and invoices that had been paid during the last week of December 2003. I had not taken the time to enter those into my record book. I was waiting for the opportunity to enter them at the same time as I tabulated my end of the year totals. As I thumbed through the receipts and invoices, I located the statement for the credit card that Captain Summers had asked about. The statement listed one charge, for which I had written check number 9728 on December 31, 2003, in the amount of $56.85. The charge was dated November 21, 2003, from HOSTWAY.COM WEBHOSTING...IL. This was the statement that the GBI Investigators and the Rockdale County Sheriffs Deputies had been looking for and was so interested in! They had not located it because it had been attached to the record book and for whatever reason they had decided not to take this book with them.

I sat back in my chair, ruefully shaking my head. For I now realized what must have happened—or at least a part of it, anyway.

I remembered opening this bill right after Christmas, probably as early as Friday, December 26, but certainly not any later than Monday, December 29th. The previous week, my family and I had enjoyed Christmas at Disney World in Orlando, Florida, returning on Friday, December 26th. The week before New Year's Day was a short work week. Alison and I left to spend the weekend at Amicalola Falls State Park in North Georgia on December 31st. We had returned on Sunday, January 4th. I had rushed to pay bills on Wednesday, the 31st, before we left Conyers. I simply opened the statement along with other bills I receive on a daily basis and placed them in my "bills to be paid" slot on my desk organizer.

I began to recall that on Saturday, December 6, 2003, my office manager, Debbie Boyd, and my nephew, Mike Phillips, had met me at my office to discuss the possibility of opening a website for my legal research firm, Southern Courthouse Ventures.

Mike had experience in opening and establishing websites. I was unfamiliar with that industry, so I was interested in hiring him to open one for my business. He and Debbie met early to discuss some of the aspects of our business that would match a website that she and I had been discussing for several weeks. I joined their conversation around noon to see what was developing. We sat in my office for about an hour discussing the basic needs and dynamics involved in developing a website. Mike explained that there were three or four major web-host companies that offered a variety of programs with different types of benefits for businesses. Trusting in Mike's judgment explicitly and realizing he comprehended our needs and desires as far as a website for my company, I authorized him and Debbie to select the best web-host company that would offer the best service. Further, I told them they could go ahead and contract with the web-host company and that I wanted Mike to build our site. Mike said he wanted to investigate other companies and that he would get back with me before instigating a contract. I told him that was unnecessary and to go ahead and get started. Both Debbie and Mike stayed a while longer and discussed the website after I left the office.

When I opened the credit card statement, some three weeks later and saw "HOSTWAY.COM," my initial thought was, "Well, I guess Mike and Debbie have set up our web account for my company." I didn't stop to think about the fact that this was my PERSONAL credit card account and not the BUSINESS credit card account that Debbie was authorized to use for business charges. I simply saw the charge, thought it was legitimate and placed it in my "to-be-paid" slot. Then on December 31st, I PAID THE BILL! Later, I learned that neither Mike nor Debbie had contacted a web-host company. They had decided to wait until after the first of the New Year, 2004, to give them more time to better develop the items for the website. When I wrote the check on December 31, 2003, I did not realize that I was paying for an illegal child pornography website that someone else had established, having stolen my name and personal information.

As I sat in my chair, my mind still registering shock and dismay, remembering the series of events that I had knowledge of, I just could not feel any sense of relief or confidence. It seemed that from the deepest depths of my soul, for the first time in my life, I was beginning to feel nothing but dread and fear.

That's when I was finally able to hit my knees at my personal altar and pour my heart out to my God. I realized that the only true source of comfort is in the strong and mighty tower of the Name of the Lord, and my spirit was running toward it for my very life.

CHAPTER 4

TUESDAY, JANUARY 6, 2004 THE ACCUSED

I awoke Tuesday morning about six o'clock after only sleeping about two hours—and that very lightly. My mind had continued to race in a hundred different directions during the night and I could not settle on any one conclusion concerning my situation. Throughout the night, I spiritually crawled to God's mighty throne of grace, although I was still filled with fear. I wasn't sure exactly what to ask Him for; and, even if I did, I wasn't sure exactly how to ask for it. I wasn't sure if I deserved any consideration from Him and the fear of rejection sapped my courage. On one hand, I had assurance in God because of His many blessings in the past, however, the terrible events of the day before had shaken my confidence considerably. Before rising to face the day, I folded my hands behind my head and began to thank God for the day. I told Him that I would not ask Him for anything. I just simply gave Him praise and refused to ask Him for more help than I had asked Him the previous night. While I'm sure He accepted my praise, not asking Him for further help was a foolish and regrettable mistake.

After getting up and dressing, I didn't eat any breakfast, for all of my appetite had left me. I sat at my library desk and reviewed the papers I was taking to my attorney that morning. I placed them in a black cloth satchel, carried them to my car and left home about 8:30 A.M. It was a cold, windy winter's day with the temperature in the 20's. I drove to old town Conyers where Gary's office was located, arriving about 8:50 A.M. After parking in the city parking lot, I sat for a few minutes listening to the news on the radio then emerged from my car to walk in a cold breeze to my attorney's office.

Gary Moore wasn't there and did not arrive until about 9:15 A.M. During the wait, I walked up and down the block, looking in the store windows. Even though it was very cold, I was able to ignore the weather. I was wearing a sweater, heavy overcoat and gloves, a scarf and an Irish golf hat. However, it wasn't the clothing that kept me from feeling the cold; I believe it was my fear of the unknown.

Gary's office is located within sight of the Rockdale County Courthouse. I had been inside that old courthouse innumerable times performing various legal researches. I could not help but wonder as I looked at it, if a trial for my very life would not be taking place inside of that old building very soon.

Soon Gary arrived and we sat in his office. Gary reviewed the various bank and credit card statements that I had brought and expressed satisfaction that I was able to locate two years worth of records so quickly. He was particularly pleased that I had located the credit card statement that Captain Summers had wanted to see and was unable to locate during their search. I told him about Debbie Boyd and Mike Phillips and the explanation about the web-host company charge. He read the law aloud from which the search warrant was issued and we reviewed the fact that I had not purchased, ordered or solicited any child pornography. Plus the fact that I was not in any way involved with the creation or operation of an illegitimate website. Again, Gary told me that I was not to answer any questions or to make any statements without his consent, except to explain the location of the credit card statement they were seeking. We walked to Gary's automobile and drove to the Rockdale County Sheriffs Department arriving about 10:00 A.M.

Captain Warren Summers again met us in the lobby area and escorted us back to Interview Room One. Gary told Captain Summers that we were giving him two years worth of bank and credit card statements from which he could make all of the copies that he needed. As I handed Captain Summers the two separate stacks of paper, I explained that the particular credit card statement they were seeking was on top. He studied the statement for a moment and then asked, "Where had you kept this?"

I replied, "It was in my bookkeeping pad located in the upper right hand drawer of my desk. It was clipped together with other paid receipts."

I further explained that I had kept it there to be entered into my ledger at a later time. He then asked me to explain the web-hosting company charge.

I looked at Gary who nodded at me. I proceeded to give Captain Summers the same explanation that I had given Gary earlier that morning in his office. Captain Summers gave me his full attention while I told him about Debbie and Mike and the attempt to create a website for my legal research firm.

When I finished, Captain Summers took my files, had someone make copies of them and then returned shortly with a female detective. He explained that she had been one of the officers involved with the search warrant yesterday and that she would be following up on the information I had just given him. She asked me to confirm the two names, Debbie Boyd and Mike Phillips. She told me that she remembered meeting Debbie the day before and asked if Debbie could be reached at my office. I confirmed that she could. She asked me if I had a telephone number for Mike Phillips, and I answered, "No." I did tell her that Debbie would be able to provide her with Mike's contact information, as he was Debbie's son.

The female detective told me that she appreciated the cooperation she had received yesterday at my home and office. Before she left the room, she thanked me for the information that I had provided.

After she exited, Gary informed Captain Summers that I was prepared to take a polygraph examination concerning the establishment of the child pornography website. Captain Summers replied that he was not ready to conduct such an examination but that he may want to do so at a later time. He then conducted us back to the lobby and told us to wait there while the other officer finished photocopying the records I had brought.

Gary and I waited silently in the lobby until another deputy returned my financial records. We then walked out and back to his automobile. As we drove back to his office, Gary expressed that he thought the interview went well and the fact that I had been so "forthcoming," by providing even more information than they had requested, played well also. Captain Summers and the female detective had both commented that Alison and my staff had been very cooperative and were even nice to the investigators the previous day. Putting all of that together, Gary said he felt that we had done all and as well as we could do.

There were two things bothering me, really bothering me. The first was that as we stood up to leave the interview room, Captain Summers said that while he appreciated me providing them with the financial information, "You will still be held fully responsible for anything we find on your computers." Gary then told him what I had told Gary earlier about the numerous pop-ups and advertisements of all types of pornography, including child pornography. Captain Summers again repeated that they and the GBI would thoroughly examine the computer hard drives and that, "Anything we find on them, Mr. Reynolds will be held fully responsible."

Secondly, Gary had requested that my main office computer, the one named "Matthew," be returned as soon as possible. Captain Summers stated that he would forward our request but that he did not promise any fast results. That also bothered me.

So, there I was. Not only was I without vital machinery to operate my business, but I knew they would find all of those pop-ups and advertisements of child pornography on my computers. I just didn't have a clue as to what the investigators would do and what laid in store for me down the road. When I expressed this to Gary, he said for me to try my best not to worry about something that had not yet happened. However, he added that he knew that that was easier said than done.

CHAPTER 5

THURSDAY, JANUARY 8, 2004 THE ACCUSED

After leaving Gary's office Tuesday morning, I went back to my office and arranged my work for the rest of the day. I sat down with my office staff and reviewed recent occurrences, again apologizing profusely. Then we discussed how we would keep up with our legal research requests until such time we had our computers returned or I bought new ones and rebuilt our system.

I then made the most important telephone call of the whole situation. I called my good friend and long time pastor, Dr. Jerry A. Patterson. Just as Alison had explained to him earlier, I told him the tangled tale of events from Monday and from earlier that morning. He gave me words of assurance and pledged to help me in any manner that he could. We had known each

other for almost forty years, and I had worked intimately with him in his ministry, so those were not
empty words he was speaking. For a long time, he
and I had met for breakfast on Thursday mornings,
and I confirmed that I would see him again that
Thursday.

THE DOCTOR

I later spoke with Jim and we set up an appointment. I still did not know enough about what had
transpired to make any sense of what was going on,
however, I did sense that they knew the seriousness
of these kinds of events. I could not imagine that the
charges I had heard mentioned could possibly have
any basis in reality. It went against everything I knew
about Jim, and I had known him a long, long time.

I shared what I knew with my wife, and later
she and I both went to prayer on behalf of Jim and
Alison. Neither of us ever believed the accusations
could be true. My wife and I both believed this was
some terrible mistake and would become apparent in
the continuing investigation.

THE ACCUSED

I then left my office and drove to a couple of area
county courthouses and performed legal research,
keeping to myself. I spent a quiet evening at home
but had another restless night.

Early Wednesday morning Alison drove to
Dr. Patterson's office and met with him. Besides

pastoring Faith Tabernacle Church, he is also a noted clinical psychologist. Alison discussed her feelings, her uncertainties and her fear of the legal ramifications involving the accusations. Dr. Patterson advised, for her own protection, that she consult with another attorney, other than Gary Moore, to provide her with representation in case there was further legal fallout in the future. They also arranged for another meeting for Saturday morning at which I would be present. Later, Alison visited the law offices of Robert Mumford where they consulted with her, however, she decided to wait and see what was going to happen before proceeding with any further legal representation. She was going to depend upon prayer for the best.

THE WIFE

Dr. Patterson helped me buy some time for my mind and to see what the facts were before panicking and packing a suitcase. I had seen some of the unpleasant pop-ups on our office computer screens and when the law enforcement officials showed up, my mind immediately recalled them. It was difficult to understand what was happening, why it was happening and what should I do, if anything.

THE DOCTOR

Alison entered my office, poised and stately. As she greeted me, she drew a deep breath and said, "Well...where do we start with this?"

We both smiled at her humor in adversity and started our first talk together.

THE ACCUSED

That same Wednesday, I again worked with Sean Peacock while continuing his legal research training. Basically, I was trying to stay very busy, hoping that activity would keep my mind off of the harrowing situation I was facing.

As was our usual custom, on Thursday morning I met Dr. Patterson at the Conyers Holiday Inn restaurant for breakfast. Over the years, I had many times asked for his advice and sage wisdom, both as a minister and a friend, and he had never given me bad counsel. During our short meal, I further explained in detail the events from earlier in the week. I also described the numerous pop-ups, advertisements and spam that we had suffered from over the past couple of years and my futile attempts to deal with them. I told him I felt totally responsible for the situation and was remorseful for not dealing with it more effectively in the past. I also told him that upon seeing some of the depictions from the advertisements that I had actually become physically ill. My stomach had churned and I had felt nauseated at some of the pictures I had seen. My failures and shortcomings had brought this shameful state of affairs to a head, and I was not only concerned for my fate but very concerned for my wife, family and business.

Dr. Patterson expressed that while Alison was understandably upset, she was not planning to abandon me. Instead, she appeared to be determined to stay with me and face this situation together. We discussed the legal dynamics, and he suggested ways that I might protect my family in case there were further consequences. He agreed to meet with me more than just our usual breakfast meeting which was for our friendship sake. He felt I might need counseling as events unfolded and his professional expertise would be at my disposal. I gladly agreed, and he said he felt strongly that Alison would be happy and supportive about that.

Leaving our breakfast, I proceeded to do one of the hardest things I thought I could ever do, and that was to inform my two daughters as to what had occurred. My eldest daughter, Joy, had recently opened a new jewelry store in Conyers named, "The Joy of Jewelry," a very appropriate name I would say. She had just opened the store the previous September, co-owning it with her mother, Jennifer. My youngest daughter, Jenna, also worked in the store.

I entered the store and Jenna greeted me with a hug. I asked her if Joy was around and she said that Joy was attending a Conyers Chamber of Commerce meeting but should return shortly. I told Jenna about the events earlier in the week, and as I was finishing, Joy walked in. I retold the story, emphasizing that I had never been involved with any kind of website, much less an illegal one.

While talking with Joy and Jenna, Alison beeped over on my cell phone. When I responded to her, Alison told me that I was to give Gary Moore a call. She said she thought the GBI was going to release one of our computers. I called Gary, and he confirmed that "Matthew," my main computer, was being released and that it was clean. We arranged to meet at the Sheriffs Department in thirty minutes.

I told Joy and Jenna what had just occurred. They both hugged me and said they had confidence in me and that everything would work out okay. I drove to the Rockdale County Sheriffs Department building and met Gary as he pulled into the parking lot. We walked inside and Gary announced our presence to the receptionist.

In just a couple of minutes, a Sheriffs Deputy brought out "Matthew" on a hand truck. "Matthew" was one of the four computers utilized in my office, the others being named "Mark," "Luke" and "John." Gary signed the "return" form as receiver of the computer. The Deputy Sheriff rolled "Matthew" outside where Gary and I loaded it into the back of my car. As we parted, Gary said he would be in touch with me as soon as anything else developed. It would not be until January 26th that I would speak with Gary again.

While driving back to my office, I called ahead and told Robin Criswell that "Matthew" was coming home. Everybody shouted, "Great!" in the background. I took the computer back to the office, and before the day was over, my office staff had everything caught up and back to running smoothly again.

Now the waiting game began.

CHAPTER 6

MONDAY,
JANUARY 26, 2004
THE ACCUSED

During the three weeks subsequent to the seizure of my computers by the Georgia Bureau of Investigation and the Rockdale County Sheriffs Department, I pursued my regular routine. I continued to operate my legal research firm, hired and trained new employees, visited family and attended church—none of the actions that you would expect from a person guilty of criminal activity. On Saturday, January 10th, Alison and I had our first visit together with Dr. Patterson who encouraged and helped us as much as possible to prepare for an uncertain future.

THE DOCTOR

Jim and I began talking in sessions right away, and I found him in our first meeting to be somewhat disillusioned that he could be in such a situation. Jim was too realistic to ask "Why?" but emphatic in asking "How?" He understood well he had not done what he was charged with doing, so how could he be accused and how could all these things be happening?

As I mentioned earlier, I have known Jim most of my life. I have been with him in the best and worst of times. I have seen him on the mountain and in the valley. I have seen him handle praise and criticism, but I had never seen him as he was in our first meeting. With so many big things going wrong in his world, I am not sure Jim knew what to expect from his friends or family, in view of the nature of what he was being charged with. In his mind, he knew his family and friends would be there for him, but emotionally he was frightened and insecure because of the horrible things of which he was accused.

When I saw him, I embraced him. I could feel his relief, although neither of us said anything at first. Out of this embrace, the atmosphere in the room changed from uncertainty to compassion and we began to talk.

Jim explained to me all he knew of the legal aspect of what he was being charged with. He sounded serious, as well as he should have, and I took what he said just as serious. He seemed to feel confident in his selection of legal representation, and it proved to be an excellent choice. Garland Moore's hand was steady and his voice reassuring, although he never minimized the nature of the accusations or the seriousness of the overall charges.

After Jim explained about the legal aspect of his dilemma, he continued to tell me what he could about how this whole thing started. Again, because of the confidentiality of counseling, I will not reveal everything, except to say that nothing he ever said lent any credibility to the accusations brought against him—not one thing. Jim explained to me about the pop-ups on his computer and how he generally dealt with them. He also explained how on occasions, for various reasons, he found himself entangled with some undesirable site, due to a pop-up. I felt he was completely honest in what he told me about this.

Jim was embarrassed and humiliated by the accusations and charges brought against him, so much so that he wondered if he could be guilty of something he knew he did not do. I have never seen anyone more shaken by their own reality, nor more confused in their efforts to make sense of it. He simply could not believe this was happening to him. I knew how he felt because I shared his feelings.

Through the fog of disbelief, I tried to bring Jim and I back to the reality of the incongruous and absurd and how we should deal with it.

THE ACCUSED

The next day, I attended services at Faith Tabernacle Church located on Ralph Road in Conyers. Admittedly, I felt self-conscious knowing that the word about the investigation must have been known by just about everyone there. However, the conversation before the service began was both encouraging and supportive. Until that service, I had still been reticent in approaching God with my needs, giving my all to Him. I had basically and simply said, "You know my needs," without expressing full confidence in Him, "who knows the feelings of our infirmities." The atmosphere of praise and worship as the service began made it easier for me to feel confident in approaching the Lord and confessing my need of His grace and mercy. That's one of the greatest attributes of this church, the people worshipping around you help to create the atmosphere of trust and confidence in Jesus Christ that you need. When you begin to pray and worship yourself, that same atmosphere seems to create a vacuum inside of you that you know only Christ Himself can fill. I made peace with my God, but I still needed to make peace within myself.

The following Saturday, January 17th, Alison and I met again with Dr. Patterson, and Alison showed what a strong woman she is. She reiterated with strong words of her desire that she and I battle this legal situation together and face our uncertain future with faith. Knowing that she was with me, that God was real and that Dr. Patterson stood with me increased my confidence that things would work out.

Alison and I met with Dr. Patterson again on Saturday, the 24th. I had not heard from Gary Moore anything further concerning the charges against me nor of any progress to obtain back my other computers. The silence was troubling, and I wanted some kind of action from some direction. I had proceeded with my usual schedule, but the unknown still affected my nerves. I was still worried about the last statement from Captain Summers when he said that whatever was found on my computers, I would be held "fully responsible." I was still highly suspicious at the more than occasional drive-by of a Rockdale County Sheriffs car through my neighborhood and suspected that my telephones had been tapped. I did not really fear any of these activities. If the authorities wanted to watch my house or listen to my telephone conversations—fine! All they would hear or observe were the normal, everyday conversations and routines of a typical, hardworking American family.

Dr. Patterson said that no news usually meant good news. However, in two days, the news would change my life forever.

THE WIFE

With Dr. Patterson to talk with and to work through the different and various concerns that I had, I was able to come to the decision to stay. Once I made that decision firm and final, I immediately felt okay and confident. Jim wasn't guilty of what the authorities were accusing him of, and I was going to stick by him all the way.

THE DOCTOR

From the first time we met and all through our subsequent sessions, Alison Reynolds remained steadfast in her determination to see Jim through this ordeal, as well as remaining supportive in the process. She simply was not sure how to best accomplish this. She did not understand, at the onset, just how such charges could be brought against someone without solid, credible evidence. At the same time, she could not believe such evidence could possibly exist. She was unable to accept that the man she loved and trusted could ever involve himself in such horrible things. However, the reality was, she and Jim were going to have to deal with this unbelievable situation; and of course, they would do it.

THE OFFICE MANAGER

As I began to recall the ordeal (that's how I refer to it), I realize now how naïve I was. I remember thinking, "Tell the truth, provide what is asked for, and the fearful situation will be over." As it turned out, that was only half true. The fear did disappear. Jim and I, along with many others, vowed to behave as God would want us to. In return, He let us enter the city of refuge. In this place, no matter how bad things were, we knew there was a net beneath us…a firm foundation, the foundation of Life.

THE ACCUSED

On Monday, January 26th, I worked in several area courthouses as I normally do. After returning to my office and finishing up my paperwork, Alison and I enjoyed a light supper and then went into our living room where we settled to relax, by enjoying a Martin Lawrence movie entitled "National Security." Alison had worked all day in the living room packing boxes with books and other educational materials to send to her daughter, Virginia, a teacher and college student living in Charlotte, North Carolina. While the movie played, she continued to pack a few more things while sitting on the floor. When she finished, she sat on the couch to enjoy the rest of the movie.

At approximately 8:00 P.M. there was a knock on our front door. Alison turned her head toward the door and said, "I wonder who that could be."

I arose from my chair and went to the front door, opening it. Gary Moore was standing on the porch and quietly asked, "Can I come in?"

I said, "Sure," and shook his hand. As he entered our living room, he saw the boxes that Alison had been packing scattered about and he asked, "Ya'll aren't moving, are you?"

Alison laughed and explained what she had been working on during the day. She then excused herself and went upstairs. I invited Gary to sit on our couch while I sat down on an ottoman.

Gary's voice is usually very low in a normal conversation and he started talking in what I thought was an even lower tone. I am somewhat hard of hearing anyway and certain tones are difficult for me to understand. So as he spoke, I leaned closer to him and asked him to repeat what he had just said. Honestly, I thought I had heard him correctly, but somehow I thought if he repeated what he had just said that the impact on my heart and mind would not be the same.

I was wrong.

Gary did repeat himself and said exactly the same thing.

"I got a telephone call from the Rockdale County Sheriffs Department and they have issued a warrant for your arrest. You've been charged with twelve counts of possessing child pornography."

For a moment, the silence felt so heavy, so deafening in my ears, that I thought someone must have removed all of the air in the room. I had turned the movie off when Gary came into the living room, and now all I could hear was the rapid beating of my heart pounding in my head. My first thought was, "This is not real." My second thought was, "Oh my God. What's going to happen to me now?" I felt thoroughly numb. I felt totally overwhelmed and completely distraught. I couldn't accept or believe that this was happening to me. I had never been arrested before in my life, and now I was being charged for the most horrendous of crimes that I could think of. I could imagine people thinking, "Well, he had those pictures. I wonder what else he's been doing." Suddenly I had a score of other thoughts run through my mind, but it was Gary who brought me back to reality and kept me focused on the issue at hand.

Gary explained to me that bail would be set the next day. He asked me if I could have cash ready or if someone I knew would offer a property bond. I told him I thought so on both counts. He then said that the Sheriffs Department was not going to come out to my house to arrest me, if I would voluntarily surrender the next day at their office. He said they didn't want to embarrass me by placing me in handcuffs in front of my family, neighbors and employees. I told him I would surrender, and he said if I would meet him at his office at 1:00 P.M. he would take me to the Rockdale County Jail and make sure I was handled properly. He said that if I were able to make bond that I would not have to spend the night incarcerated. He said he would do all that he could to expedite my release.

I asked him about the newspapers and if my arrest could be kept out of them. He said he would request suppression if it were available in this case, however, he thought it would be difficult to keep the news of my arrest out of the local journals. He felt the local county newspapers, *The Rockdale Citizen* and *The Newton Citizen* would probably publish my arrest, but he said he would do what he could to keep press coverage to a minimum.

Gary assured me that he would stay with me throughout the process and would do all that he could to minimize publicity of my being arrested. I was left in a stunned state of mind as Gary walked out and back across the street to his home.

After I closed the front door and locked it, I placed my head against the door panel and prayed, "Lord, I need your mercy and grace. Please help me." Alison's voice calling me from upstairs caused me to pull away from the door and make my way to our bedroom.

Alison was sitting up in the bed and asked me, "What did Gary have to say?"

I sat down on the bed and told her that the Sheriffs Department had issued a warrant for my arrest and that I would have to surrender myself the next day. She could tell that emotions were overwhelming me, and she moved over and held me tightly.

"Oh, Jim," she said, "we'll make it through this. It's okay." I don't know if she knew she was being prophetic or not but the word "through" would have tremendous meaning in the future.

As much as I was upset over the thought of being arrested and all that it entailed, I was more over-whelmed by this expression of love from Alison. I then simply gave in to my emotions and began to weep as I had not wept in a long time. She held me for several minutes until I regained my composure. I physically shook my head violently and then said, "Okay. Let's see what we've got to do now."

I guess all of my professional abilities kicked in, and she and I began to enumerate the things we needed to work out. The first thing I did was call my friend, Dr. Patterson. I reached him at home and informed him of the arrest warrant. I then asked him if he would be able to help me with making my bond using some property he owned. He unhesitatingly agreed. I explained that if we gave a cash bond, the money would be forfeited no matter the outcome of the case. My preference would be to utilize those funds for the attorney fees I knew were accruing. He said he understood perfectly and that he would start early the next morning preparing the papers to secure a property bond on a house he owned. I told him I was so sorry that I had called on him and for this mess but that I truly appreciated his kind help. He said, "You've helped me when I've needed it. When I needed a friend to talk with, you were there. I'm glad I can help."

His words were very comforting and I realized just how valuable it was to have a friendship that had lasted nearly forty years. Only later would I learn just how valuable our friendship was, and is.

Alison and I then sat and talked about our business and who else we should call. As we discussed these subjects, I was constantly saying to myself, "This will just be for one day."

All of our discussions and decisions were based on the idea that I would be arrested and released on the same day. Alison asked about calling my mother and my children and I responded that I would rather wait until after I returned and contact them myself. I could then give them full details and they would hear it directly from me. I said that I would call all of them Tuesday evening after I was bonded out. I thought it might soften the blow if I told them myself.

I tried to sound confident that everything would go as smoothly as possible and that I would call her as soon as everything was finished. Alison consistently assured me that she loved me and that she would stick by me throughout the ordeal. I think her favorite line was, "We'll get through this together." Although my emotions and thoughts were greatly shaken, her words gave me comfort and peace on the inside.

CHAPTER 7

TUESDAY, JANUARY 27, 2004-DAYTIME
THE ACCUSED

Alison and I arose early to a cool, crisp, but sunny Tuesday morning, dressing to go to a doctor's appointment Alison had made for us the previous week. We had discussed the night before about whether or not to keep this appointment for a regular physical examination and decided to keep it. Our physician, Dr. Earl Thurmond, has an office located on Panola Road near Atlanta, Georgia. It's often difficult to match schedules with this popular doctor, and Alison had set the appointment not realizing the turn of events that would occur.

Being a cold morning, I dressed in a sweater and overcoat. We got to Dr. Thurmond's office a little early, but his nurses proceeded to check me in ahead of schedule. In his usual quiet and mild manner, Dr.

Thurmond came into the examination room asking me how I had been doing.

"My physical health has been fine," I told him, "but my emotional state is in a total mess. You won't believe what has been happening to me."

I proceeded to unburden myself about how the Georgia Bureau of Investigation and the Rockdale County Sheriffs Department had seized five of my computers because they thought I owned and operated a child pornography website. And that even though I was completely innocent of those charges, I was being held responsible for the images found on my computer. Additionally, there was not any evidence showing I purchased or ordered the images nor had I e-mailed anyone or entered into any chat rooms. Dr. Thurmond expressed shock at such allegations and asked what he could do to help. I told him I could probably use a strong sleeping medicine along with refilling my regular prescriptions. He checked my blood pressure and it read 128 over 82. "Pretty good," he said, explaining that he had expected it to read much higher considering the stress I was enduring.

Dr. Thurmond advised that I do all that I could to not overstress concerning this situation. He expressed concern that my previous heart trouble had developed from stress. He stated his apprehension that my present worries would do the same thing. He also told about his problems with spam and pop-ups and of others that he knew who had experienced the same. He was amazed that this serious situation had developed against me. I told him about the internet watch group and the apparent theft of my identity and credit card information. I also told him how my attorney had explained that just a little bit of evidence can warrant an arrest but it takes a whole lot more to bring about a trial or a conviction. He again expressed a desire to help me any way that he could, and I thanked him for his concern. I left his office feeling that at least I was apparently healthy and could physically endure whatever lay ahead. I also felt that spiritually I was prepared to endure whatever came. I wasn't so sure of my emotional health, though.

When Dr. Thurmond finished with Alison's physical examination, she drove us back to Conyers and we stopped at the Cracker Barrel Restaurant for an early lunch. Neither one of us had eaten before going to the doctor's office. I was to meet Gary Moore at his office at 1:00 P.M. Alison ordered breakfast, and I ordered chicken and rice soup with cornbread. An ironic thought ran through my mind; I felt like I was eating my last meal. Alison and I did not talk much, however, her conversation was encouraging and loving, whereas I was lost in my own thoughts. I was feeling a certain premonition that everything was not going to be as simple as we hoped it would be, but I could not discern why I felt that way.

After lunch, we drove back home and by then it was time for me to leave. We discussed her taking me to Gary's office, but I told her I felt Gary would complete the bond process quickly and that I would return soon afterwards. Shortly after I drove away, Alison received a telephone call from our daughter-in-law, Maggie Rolling. Maggie lived in Dayton,

Ohio, with our son, AJ, and our granddaughter, Misty Jane. AJ was in the United States Air Force and stationed at Wright-Patterson Air Force Base. Maggie told Alison that AJ and Rob, AJ's younger brother, were planning to leave that day for a ski trip to Colorado and were going to leave her and Misty Jane there alone. Maggie asked if Alison could fly up for the rest of the week and keep Misty while Maggie worked. Alison truly loves her granddaughter and usually would travel to see her without giving it much thought. Realizing the seriousness of our situation, but feeling the need to help Maggie if she could, Alison told Maggie she would talk with me and call her back.

I drove to downtown Conyers and parked my car in the city parking lot. I walked to Gary's office where his receptionist directed me to his rear office. As I walked back to his office, I met Hyrum Pierce, former Judge and now an attorney who maintains a law office with Gary Moore. We greeted each other, as we have known each other for over twenty years. I proceeded to Gary's office and took a seat across from his desk.

Gary handed me the arrest warrant and told me to read it as he pulled out a law book from his extensive library. The arrest warrant stated that I was to be arrested for "Sexual Exploitation of Children" and a description of the images located on one of my computers was listed. There were twelve separate warrants describing twelve different pictures found on my computers. I only read the top one and scanned the others. They were all similar. I began to feel physically uncomfortable and nauseated. I noticed my hands trembling as I placed the warrants back on Gary's desk.

Gary then proceeded to read to me the law under which I was being arrested; basically, the possession of illegal images. The law under which I was being arrested was located in Volume 16, Book 12, Article 100, Section B and Paragraph 8, which states:

"It is unlawful for any person knowingly to possess or control any material which depicts a minor or a portion of a minor's body engaged in any sexually explicit conduct."

He read to me that each count in the warrants subjected me from five to twenty years in prison and a fine up to $100,000 for each count. Quickly calculating in my head, I was facing, if indicted and convicted, a sixty to two hundred and forty year sentence in prison AND a fine of 1.2 million dollars. For a second I thought I would pass out. It was unbelievable. Again, my mind was blank and I felt like I was going into shock. I felt like this was totally unreal and could not be happening to me. I was hoping for an out of body experience where I could just watch what was going to happen and not be involved in it.

Gary advised me that the charges, while a felony, did not require any minimum time in prison. Because of my previous clean record, any sentence would probably be served on probation. He felt my lack of any prior problems with the law would mitigate any punishment. He typed out a bond request, leaving the amount space empty. He told me that the arrest warrants had not established a bail and that he was going to see a judge to set a bond amount. Before leaving, Gary called Dr. Patterson and asked if he was ready to get a property bond, if needed. Dr. Patterson confirmed that he had his property records in order.

Gary said we were to go to the Sheriffs Department at 2:00 P.M. so I was free to go out if I wanted to while he visited a judge. I left his office and went to the local library and sat in their reading room glancing through news magazines. I was not in any kind of mood for any serious reading. I returned to Gary's office ahead of Gary and sat in his office until he returned. Soon he entered and informed me that my bail had been set at $5,000 per warrant. $60,000!!! Once more my already shaken emotions suffered another stunning and shocking blow.

Gary again called Dr. Patterson and told him the amount of the bond. Dr. Patterson replied that he would proceed to the Newton County Sheriffs Department and would contact Gary as soon as possible. The property that Dr. Patterson was going to utilize for my bond was located in Newton County, which neighbored Rockdale County. Dr. Patterson would have to go through the Newton County Sheriffs Department to have the property applied to the bond, and then that information would be transferred to the Rockdale County Sheriffs Department. Gary didn't think there would be any problems with that.

I left my car in the city parking lot and Gary drove us in his car to the Rockdale County Sheriffs Department. Alison telephoned me on my cell phone while I was riding beside Gary and told me of the situation with Maggie and Misty Jane. She asked what I thought about her flying to Dayton. A part of me didn't want her to leave, but I decided that was selfish of me and told her it was quite all right for her to go. I knew she wanted to go; she loves that granddaughter more than anything else in the world. She expressed anxiety about the bonding process, but I assured her it would work out all right. She said she would take an early evening flight and that she would call me later in the evening to find out what happened.

Unknown to me, I would not be able to speak to her again until Thursday.

When we arrived, we sat in the Sheriffs Department lobby for about twenty minutes. A Sheriff's Department Lieutenant came in followed shortly by a female agent of the Georgia Bureau of Investigation. They asked Gary to join them in their office, and he told me to wait there for him to return.

I sat alone in the lobby for approximately an hour and a half. At two different times, a couple of other folks came and sat near, but we did not speak to each other. Otherwise, I sat there alone, nervous and afraid.

While I waited, a jail trustee, dressed in the orange coveralls of the prison, came through cleaning up. I tried to imagine what it would feel like to wear those orange coveralls. I couldn't. This was the first time that I experienced the jailhouse orange.

Orange.

Always orange.

Meanwhile, Gary was being shown the evidence gathered by the Rockdale County Sheriffs Department investigators and the GBI. In part, Gary asked if the website had been in any way linked to me. He was told, "No." He asked if money had been shown being moved around to purchase pictures or to establish a website. Again, he was told, "No." He asked if they had any indication of unusual deposits or electronic transfer of funds linked to me and they said, "No." He asked if they had been able to trace the source of the twelve images that I had been charged with illegally possessing. The response he received was that they did not care where the images had come from; they simply were satisfied in charging me with possession of those images and besides, there were hundreds more that had been located. Gary then told them that HE was concerned with the source of the images and that he would gain custody of the computers or their hard drives so that his computer experts could track down exactly where those particular images had come from. He would also determine if those images were purchased by me or someone else or whether or not they were the result of pop-ups or from some other source. Apparently fretful about the time and cost that a longer and more extensive investigation would incur, the agents then told Gary that if he was going to do that, then they were going to interview and interrogate every one of my family, my employees, current and past, and every one of my neighbors and friends.

Gary then said, "That's fine. And you can begin right here, right now, with me. Ask me anything that you want to about Jim Reynolds."

They asked him why they should do that.

"Because I have lived across the street from him and his family for ten years. Ask me anything you want to."

Of course, they were not prepared with any questions, but nevertheless, the charges stood and the arrest proceeded.

After talking with the agents and reviewing the evidence, Gary joined me in the lobby and sat with me for about fifteen minutes. He explained his discussion with the agents and said he would go with me to the jail. After I was booked into the jail, he would contact Dr. Patterson and assist him in any way that he could. We were joined by the Sheriff's Department Lieutenant, who asked us to follow her.

As she exited the door in front of us, I asked Gary, "Why do I feel like a sheep being led to the slaughter?"

Gary said that he would take care of things and for me not to answer any questions except the basic information that they would need to process me. We stepped out of the Sheriffs Department office into the cool setting sun of this Tuesday afternoon. It was approximately 5:40 P.M. and the shadows were long and the wind was up as we walked toward the Rockdale County Detention Center. The Lieutenant led the way with Gary right behind her, and I followed about three steps behind. I kept my hands in my pockets and my head down; depression is not the word to describe what I was feeling. It was about one hundred yards from the Sheriffs Office to the jail entrance, but it wasn't far enough, as far as I was concerned.

Up to this point I had not spoken a single word except to my attorney. I know I can be fairly talkative and can hold my own in just about any conversation, but this circumstance that I found myself in was totally foreign and alien to me. As we stepped into the reception area of the jail, we were confronted with a huge metal door that slid to the side. I believe there were metal detectors beside the doorway because the Lieutenant turned to me and asked, "You don't have any weapons—guns or knives—on you, do you?"

I simply shook my head and said, "No, ma'am." Here I was, probably old enough to be this officer's father or even grandfather and I was saying, "Yes, ma'am," and "No, ma'am," to her. I had determined long before that none of the legal authorities would have any reason to judge me as being anything less than cooperative, courteous and compliant.

We walked down a short walkway through a door and into another room that was long and narrow. A shelf occupied the full length of the wall along the right side, and there was another doorway in the left side wall. Straight ahead was a glass partition containing a doorway that led to a parking area to the rear of the jail. As the Lieutenant led me to the shelf, Gary said he was leaving to call Dr. Patterson and that he would see me later that evening. The Lieutenant began to ask me some personal questions, fill out a jail form and began to itemize my belongings.

After identifying me, she asked if I understood the charges, and I replied, "Yes, ma'am." She then told me she had to go inside the jail to get a male officer, but before she could do that, she had to handcuff me. She led me to the opposite side where a railing ran along part of the wall. On the railing hung several pairs of handcuffs. She took my arm and clicked the handcuffs one notch on my wrist. She actually apologized for having to do that but said it was regulation.

She walked through the doorway that led into the jail and left me standing there alone, hand-cuffed to the railing. This was surreal. I was actually HANDCUFFED!! I wanted someone to come up to me and say, "Okay. The joke's over. You can go home now." But I was held fast to the railing, and I knew this was not going to be a joke. I looked outside the glass partition and saw that the sun was finally setting for the day. However, there was still just enough light for me to see a distance, and a big wish swelled up inside of me. I would give anything to be able to walk outside and just keep walking to escape this humiliation. Before I could gather my thoughts, a male deputy came out and released me. I had been handcuffed for probably less than a minute but already it felt like another lifetime.

The deputy began to ask me the same questions I had been asked previously, checking them off of the form he was carrying. When he asked me about any prescribed medications that I was taking, I could only remember the names of three of the six that I was to take on a regular basis. I guess my nervousness made me forgetful. He then placed my overcoat, hat, shawl, billfold, belt, watch and keys into a large plastic bag labeled with my name. He then led me into the office of the jail.

I walked through the door, and to my left was an open office area with several officers working on computers, sitting behind consoles and beside filing cabinets. A high counter separated them from where I was standing. To my right was a restroom and the holding cell. The deputy who had led me inside motioned for me to move toward the holding cell and ordered me to stand by the doorway. I stood there while he gave my information and belongings to other officers behind the tall counter. As I stood there, many of the other officers stared at me. I simply stood still, doing my best to ignore them.

Shortly thereafter, the deputy came back and unlocked the holding cell, ordering me inside. This holding cell was about seven foot by fifteen foot. I know because I measured it as I walked around it. One long bench with a very thin pad lined the back wall. The bench was permanently attached to the wall. The bench held enough room for maybe four people to sit. A combination sink and commode made of stainless steel sat at the end of the bench. Opposite the bench was a narrow window for the officers to observe the holding cell. There was also a small window in the door.

There were three men already in the cell when I entered. They slid down the bench and made room for me to sit on the end next to the sink-commode combo. They all said, "Hey," and I answered back the same. When one of them asked what I was "in for," I simply ignored the question. I picked up a copy of the *Jail Rulebook* and began reading it. The other three men resumed their conversation among themselves. In about ten minutes, the cell door opened and an inmate entered carrying supper trays.

Each of us was given a tray with baked chicken and black-eyed peas. There were three other items, but I just don't remember what they were. I looked at my tray and I simply could not eat a thing. The least of my interests was food at that time. The other three fellows were digging in, one saying he had not eaten since the previous night. I offered them my tray. They took it with a, "thank you," and divided it among themselves. They seemed to appreciate me sharing my food with them. This was the first time that I witnessed the near obsession with food many of the prisoners have. This experience would serve me again in the coming days.

While my three fellow inmates continued eating, the cell door opened again and I was called outside. I was ordered by a deputy to stand on a black square on the floor next to the holding cell wall. I was then told to remove my glasses. They didn't tell me to smile when they took my "front" photo nor when they took the "side" view. I don't know if they knew or if they even cared that they were taking the photographs that would be flashed across the country and around the world.

CHAPTER 8

TUESDAY, JANUARY 27, 2004-EVENING THE ACCUSED

During my photo session, the deputies had removed two of the men out of the holding cell, and the remaining one had curled up on the bench with a blanket around him. The food trays had been stacked by the door awaiting pickup. Not knowing what was going to happen next filled me with anxiety and nervous energy. I kept wondering how long it was going to take to work out my bond and what time I would possibly be leaving this place. I began to pace the length of the holding cell, back and forth. As I had been for weeks now, my mind filled with prayer. I simply asked for God's protection. I didn't question God with, "What's going on?" I didn't ask, "Why?" I knew because of my own lack of conscientiousness and shortcomings that all of this was my fault, my responsibility. That, and the fact that my identity had been stolen. But I couldn't prove that sitting in a jail cell. So I just continued to ask Jesus to help me and overshadow me with His mercy.

Thank God, He did.

Again I was called out of the holding cell, and standing there was my attorney, Gary Moore. For a moment I thought, *I'm getting out of here.* But the look on Gary's face was one of discouragement, not relief. He told me that the property Dr. Patterson had submitted for my bond was not sufficient to cover the $60,000. He told me I would have to stay, but he was going to talk with Dr. Patterson a short time later. Gary said he would see me again about 10:30 P.M. that night. I then realized that I was going to spend my first night ever in jail.

Gary left and I was returned to the holding cell, overwhelmed with disappointment. Not at Gary, Dr. Patterson or anyone else, just disappointed that I was unable to bring this lurid situation to an end. When I returned to the holding cell this time, I was alone. I sat for a short time then began to pace once again. I stayed in there about fifteen more minutes when I was ordered out of the cell by a deputy sheriff. He led me to their fingerprinting equipment and processed my fingerprints. I tried to be interested in the computer that they used to fingerprint, but it was just a ruse to distract my mind. It didn't work. I was in some stage of mild shock and was moving like an automaton. I felt like I was numb in my mind and in my spirit. However, I continued to be cooperative and respectful to all of the officers. I tried to appear as pleasant as I could under the circumstances. I knew I wasn't a criminal, and I wasn't going to allow the jail atmosphere and mentality turn me into one.

Once again I returned to the holding cell where another man had been placed. This guy was a nervous talker and a mover. He sat and talked and then he stood and talked, the whole time telling me how he was arrested for hitting his wife after she had hit him first. He contended he was only defending himself. He would ask me a question and, before I could answer, he would take off on another part of his story. For the rest of the time I was with him, my only responses were nods of my head.

It was about 7:45 P.M. and I had been in the holding cell about two hours, when again, and for the last time, I was ordered outside. I was told to stand by the wall then later ordered to sit in a chair that sat next to the wall. After sitting there for about ten minutes, a deputy walked over with a one-piece orange jumpsuit, orange flip-flops, a white towel and a plastic drinking cup. He instructed me to go into a shower room situated next door, take a shower, put all of my clothes into another plastic bag, put on the orange jumpsuit and come out. I was told I could keep my underwear because they were white, but that I could not keep my socks because they were of a dark color. I entered the shower room carrying all that the deputy had given me, took a shower, put on the one-piece orange jumpsuit with the extra-long cuffs and snap-buttons on the front, slipped on the orange flip-flops, put my other clothes in the plastic

113

bag, took them out and gave them to the officer who stood waiting for me.

After he examined everything, he told me that if I lost or misplaced my plastic drinking cup I'd have to pay to get another one; same thing for my towel. Inside the cup was a small toothbrush, a small tube of toothpaste and a small deodorant-all plastic. Carrying my plastic cup along with all of the extras, I followed the deputy through two locked doors into a long hallway that was situated directly behind the open office area for the jail. We turned right and I was led to an open doorway on my right. I was told to go in, pick up a plastic bag that contained two sheets and a blanket. I was also instructed to pick up a mattress pad. I located the sheets and blanket, and then I found a mattress pad that was about three feet in width and about five feet in length. I'm five foot eleven inches tall.

The deputy then led me to a locked sliding gate that was opened after he spoke into his shoulder mike. When the door slid open, he ordered me to walk straight through this room to the next doorway and to wait there until that door opened. I was then to turn left and stop before a door with the letter "C" on it. I was to go through that door when it opened.

As I stepped through the doorway, the door rapidly slid closed behind me. To my right was a solid concrete block wall that ran toward another doorway opposite from where I stood. To my left were two small cubicles with short concrete block walls housing plastic tables and chairs. I later learned that this is where attorneys would visit their clients.

Further down was a wire cage that reached to the ceiling, holding various supplies and cleaning utensils, all under lock and key. The hallway was about fifty feet long. When I reached the other door, it quickly opened. I stepped through and entered an enclosed circular hallway that surrounded a two-story guard tower. From the guard tower, the deputies had views into each cell and section through darkened glass. The cells were to my left and went completely around the circle, surrounding the guard room. As I turned to my left and began to walk, I noticed that all of the doors were closed. It appeared that I was the only one in the circular hallway.

All of the doors were solid with no viewing glass in any of them. No windows. No openings. Overhead cameras revealed to the guards anyone that was in the hallway. After several moments, there was still no one besides me in the hallway. The cells had been closed for the night. Supper had already been served and cleaned up. I felt alone—really alone. Only slight noises could be heard coming from behind the solid metal doors. I stopped in front of the large metal door with the letter "C" stenciled on it. I stood there in my orange coveralls and orange flip-flops, holding my mattress and linens in one hand and my precious plastic drinking cup and little utilities in the other hand. I waited about three minutes, not moving a step. A voice finally spoke over a speaker and asked, "Are you waiting to enter Section C?"

I replied, "Yes, sir." In a moment, the door began to slide to the left.

While standing outside in the hallway, the noise coming from behind the door was like a low murmur. The same type of sounds could be heard coming from behind the other doors in the hallway, only fainter. It was a surprise to hear the crescendo of noise that I heard as the door slid open. Immediately as the door cracked, the loud noise of nearly forty men laughing, talking, yelling, shouting, grunting, slapping tables, and the blast of a very loud television washed over me as a cacophonous wave. As the door continued to slide further to my left, I was momentarily stunned as I tried to comprehend my new surroundings. Where do I go? Who do I talk to? Where do I put my stuff?

When I stepped through the doorway, the television high on the wall behind my right shoulder was blaring loudly. About forty men, in an area that was built to accommodate eighteen men comfortably, milled around in the midst of all that noise. All were dressed in the fashion of the day—orange jumpsuits with orange flip-flops—in a variety of appearances. Most were dressed the same as me with the jumpsuit snapped all the way up. Some had white t-shirts underneath their jumpsuits. Others had the sleeves of their jumpsuits tied around their waists baring their t-shirts or their chests.

As I stepped forward a couple of steps, one of the prisoners walked up to me and asked, "Do you have any cigarettes on ya?"

I shook my head, "No," and walked past him, still trying to acclimate myself to my surroundings. I had only taken a couple of more steps when another prisoner stopped in front of me and asked, "Did you bring any chocolate in with you?"

Again I just shook my head, "No," and began turning my eyes in all directions trying to become oriented.

Walking through the doorway of Section "C," I entered what was called the "Dayroom." This area was an open space, two stories high and made of concrete blocks. Above the doorway were the darkened glass windows through which the deputies, located in the guard tower, could observe the prisoners. The television was mounted high on the wall next to the guard window. I later learned that the guards controlled whether the television was on or off. A telephone hung on the wall beneath the television.

The two-story "Dayroom" encompassed about two-thirds of the available space inside Section "C." In the back third was located the bunk areas and showers on two floors. The bottom area housed four open cells with one open bathroom facility to serve that floor. To my left, metal stairs led up to the upper floor, which consisted of five open cells and an open bathroom facility. Each open cell had one iron metal bunk bed welded to the floor containing a top bunk for one person and a bottom bunk for another person. A small iron desk with an attached round, backless seat sat across from each bunk bed, also welded to the floor. Due to the overcrowding, the prisoners unable to secure a bunk berth were sleeping in "boats." These were "beds" made of thin but sturdy plastic, colored blue, and were about five feet eight inches long and about three feet wide. Men were sleeping in these "boats" that were either placed over storage boxes or directly on the floor.

I observed that the "Dayroom" was crowded with many men sitting at the smooth steel tables—talking, playing games of cards, checkers, chess, and reading books. There were only eighteen round, backless seats attached to the four tables that were welded to the floor. Those not able to sit in a seat were moving about, sitting on their bunks or sitting in their "boats." It appeared that there were many "boats" lined along the walls and next to the bunk beds on the lower floor. I quickly saw there was no place for me to lay down my stuff. I walked over to the metal stairs where a prisoner stood. I asked him, "Do you know where I can get a bunk?"

He shrugged his shoulders and said, "Maybe upstairs."

I turned my head and looked up the stairway. At the head of the stairs was an open cell area. Just as I glanced up, a figure lying on a top bunk raised up, looked down to where I was standing, and said, "Come on up here. There's a place right here for you next to our bunk. You'll have to get a boat though."

The man who sat up on the bunk and called me to the upper floor was named Robert Walters (not his real name), but everyone called him Charles. I later learned that Charles did not live too far from my home and had been in Section "C" for about ten days on charges involving credit cards. At the time I didn't realize the importance of meeting Charles and having him call me to the upper floor to his bunk area. I was meeting the first member of what later became known as my "Posse." I consider Charles a blessing from God in that the Lord had placed a Guardian Angel in the jail before I had even arrived!

I climbed the stairs lugging my two-inch thick mattress and carrying my other necessities. I placed them on the floor next to the dividing wall between cells. This cell was about seven feet wide and approximately twelve feet long. The bunk sat along one long wall, while the desk was along the opposite wall. Along the back wall lay a "boat" on boxes.

As I was walking up the stairs, Charles called down to another man and asked him to get a "boat" for me. At the same time, the door had slid open again and a guard standing in the doorway allowed another prisoner to step out to a storage room and return with a "boat." He handed it to a prisoner who brought it to the man Charles had called. He brought the "boat" up the stairs, telling the other man that he was going up stairs anyway and would take it. As the man carrying the "boat" reached the head of the stairs, I took the "boat" from him and set it down next to the wall with the desk. The man who had brought the "boat" up, shook my hand and introduced himself as Lars Collins (not his real name). I did not know it at the time, but Lars was the second Guardian Angel placed in that section by the mercy of God.

I placed the head of my "boat" directly against the solid side of the desk. Along my left hand side was a solid concrete block wall that extended almost to the end of my bed (boat). To my right, separated by two feet of space, was the iron bunk bed for this cell. Behind the desk and at the foot of the iron bunk were a couple of storage boxes with another "boat" sitting on top of them. Behind this was the back wall with our window view consisting of a piece of unbreakable glass about four inches wide and about four feet tall—the only window in that whole section.

I placed my thin mattress sheet over my thin mattress and placed it inside my thin "boat." I then took the thin cover sheet and tucked it in around the foot of the thin mattress pad. I pulled the thin blanket out and, realizing that I did not have a pillow, doubled it up and placed it on the end of my "boat" next to the desk. I set my plastic bag with my toiletries inside the bed next to the blanket.

I finished my "housekeeping," kicked off my orange flip-flops and sat down on my "boat." I sat with my legs crossed and my back to the wall. To my right was the desk, the other "boat" and the window view. Directly in front of me was the iron bunk bed sitting next to the other wall. Within this limited space, I was to live with three other men for the next three days.

I turned my head to the left, and that's when I noticed that just past the head of the bunk bed on the right was a large metal door. It was partially open, and I could tell that if the door was pushed closed it could only be opened with a key. I later learned that through this door was a cell for solitary confinement. Later, when the door was opened wider, I saw that there was an open area about four feet by seven feet. To the left was the observation glass for the jail guards. To the right was a metal grillwork enclosing a solitary cell approximately six feet by ten feet in space. The outer metal door was kept unlocked and partially open so that prisoners located in the area I was sitting could bring food and water to whoever was housed in the solitary area.

When I turned my head completely to the left, I was looking straight across the open space over the "Dayroom" toward the darkened glass of the guard room. There was a metal railing along the edge of the second story floor where I was sitting, theoretically to prevent falling to the floor below. There were two separate areas of lights in this section. One set of lights illuminated the "Dayroom" and another set of lights lit the open cells. The set of lights over the open cells were turned off by the guards at 11:00 P.M. and they turned them back on whenever breakfast was brought to Section "C," anytime between 4:00 A.M. and 6:00 A.M. The lights over the "Dayroom" were on 24 hours a day, seven days a week.

Unexpectedly, I noticed that the area smelled unusually clean. No foul odors or stench was evident. In fact, the area had a very sterile and disinfectant aroma in it.

After I observed my new surroundings for a few moments, Charles jumped down from the top bunk and sat across from me on the lower bunk, introducing himself. I told him I was "Jim" and asked him about the routine. He told me that basically after breakfast you did what you wanted to do until lunch. Then after lunch, you did what you wanted to do until supper. Then after supper, you did what you wanted to do until lights out. I soon learned that there were those who continued to do what they wanted to do even after the lights were out.

Charles told me that the other men in our cell were Mike Ross and Phillips (not their real names). Charles called each one of those guys over and I met them, shaking their hands and introducing myself as "Jim." Including Charles and Lars, I had now met the four guys who would become known as my "Posse." They would prove to be Guardian Angels in the coming days, though the description "angel" would be deemed by them as inappropriate.

While sitting cross-legged in my "boat" conversing with Charles, the door to our section suddenly slid opened. From where I was sitting I could clearly see the door moving. When it finished opening completely, two prison trustees rolled in a cart on wheels, followed behind by one of the jail guards. I asked Charles what was going on, and he informed me that Tuesday nights were "snack nights." All of the prisoners who had any money in their accounts at the jail were allowed to purchase chocolate candies, chips and pastries. These were dispensed to the prisoners in plastic baggies and were distributed by the calling out of names. Because I had been there only a very short time and knew I wasn't going to get anything, I didn't even rise from my "boat" while the rest of the prisoners hurried to get their goodies.

Charles walked down the stairs and got his snack baggie and came back up while eating a bag of chips. He offered me some but I declined. He sat down again on the lower bunk and began to explain that many of the guys eat their whole allotment of snacks in one sitting. He also said that several of the men would be "sugared up tonight." I guess I must have had a questioning look on my face, for he then said that there would probably be several guys up all night long.

Charles and I continued to talk for a while longer until I decided I may as well inspect my new surroundings further and stretch my legs at the same time. I invited Charles to walk with me, but he decided to jump back into the upper bunk and began reading a book. I turned to my left and walked along the metal railing, holding it with my right hand, passing four more cells on my left exactly like the one I had just left. All of them were seemingly as crowded. The railing and walkway ended at a locked door that accessed a neighboring section. Beside this door were the bathroom facilities. In an open area immediately beside the locked door sat a small steel sink with push buttons to turn on the water. Above it was a small steel mirror—no glass, just a steel reflection. Next to the sink was a short concrete wall separating the sink from one, solid steel toilet. On the other side of the toilet was the wall separating the shower area. The wall was very narrow and not very high, making it impossible for someone to be in the shower and not be seen by the guards. The shower stall consisted of one push button that would allow water to flow through the shower head for approximately three minutes. A thin shelf was attached to one shower wall to place clothes and other items.

I then walked back to the stairs and descended to the lower level and into the "Dayroom." Two men were playing chess, and I stood nearby watching them for about fifteen minutes, leaning against one of the section walls. As I stood there, I also scanned the area observing the variety of men sharing this section. Out of approximately forty men, there were eight Caucasians; about eight to ten Hispanics or Mexicans and the remainder were African-Americans. The four men in the cell I was sleeping in were white with the other four white men situated together in one of the lower cells. The Hispanics were all in the lower cells and the Blacks were located on both levels. Throughout my stay, the number of men and the demographics were constantly changing as some prisoners were removed and new ones incarcerated. I learned that Section "C" was for housing non-violent prisoners and that explained the constant turnover in "guests."

I was startled by the appearance of one of the Hispanics. He was about five foot eight and weighed approximately 250 pounds. He was completely bald- except for a short triangle of hair right in the middle of his forehead. Even more startling was the flat, cold, vivid look in his eyes. Those eyes signaled danger to me. I began to feel very vulnerable and uncomfort- able knowing that in a physical confrontation I would not be a match for such a man.

There had been two other men sitting at the table with the two chess players. Shortly after I came to stand near, one of them got up and walked off. I asked one of the men sitting there if I could sit and watch them play. He said, "Sure." His name was William (not his real name), and he was obviously a very good chess player. He asked me if I played chess, and

I told him that I knew the moves but had not played in a number of years. I told him, though, that I would enjoy playing him a game later on. I soon discovered that playing chess would allow me to endure my time in jail while helping me retain my sanity.

I stayed watching the chess games for quite some time. I resigned myself to the fact that I wasn't going anywhere soon so I may as well attempt to remain calm and get as comfortable as possible. I kept in the back of my mind that my attorney would still be working on securing my release that night, so I grasped for that serenity with all of my thoughts. When questioned as to why I was locked up, I gave vague answers like, "I've been falsely accused of a crime, but then you've heard that story before." Or I answered, "I was found with some stuff I shouldn't have had."

Lars Collins questioned me as to my profession. When I told him I was a legal researcher and owned my own company, he said, "I thought you looked like some kind of lawyer. You just look like one. I overheard someone saying they thought you were a judge or something."

I told him I wasn't an attorney or a judge but that didn't stop him or several others from consistently approaching me over the next two days with numerous legal questions of which I was not able to answer. I tried to give them the best guidance that I knew to give, and hopefully I was able to pass along some suggestions that were helpful.

Later I climbed back up the stairs and lay down in my "boat," thinking I would rest for a little while when suddenly my name was called over the loud-speaker, "James Reynolds." I answered, "Yes," and several of the other guys called out, "He's here," and the voice over the loudspeaker said, "You have a visitor." I walked down the stairs and stood at the door of my section until a guard opened it. When it opened and I stepped through the doorway into the circular hallway, I was once again alone; I did not see another person. I have to admit that I sighed, enjoying the moment. I then went toward the door that led back through to the front entrance and as it opened, a guard met me. He told me that my attorney would join me in a minute and I was to wait in that area.

I was waiting in the area that held the plastic tables and chairs. Soon Gary Moore entered the door from the jail office area. It was about 10:30 P.M. The guard asked Gary, "Do you want me to stay in here with you, Judge?"

And Gary answered, "No, I won't need you. Everything's fine."

We sat down at one of the tables and Gary explained to me that Dr. Patterson had not been able to secure the property bond on the land he was trying to put up. He said Dr. Patterson was going to try a different piece of property tomorrow; the difficulty lay in the large amount required to make bond. Gary expressed extreme disappointment at the circumstances and said he would continue to do all that he could to help Dr. Patterson and to expedite my release. Gary asked how was I doing, and I expressed to him that I was somewhat afraid of the circumstances I found myself in. Gary told me I was in a non-violent section and that I should be safe.

After our good-byes, he turned and walked out while I stood there and watched him leave, wishing I was going with him. I turned around and returned to my new home, Section "C."

For the next thirty minutes I lay in my bunk, prayed, read some in a Bible that I had located and prayed some more until the lights over our cells were turned off. I quickly discovered that it would never be completely dark in my cell. The lights over the "Dayroom" remained on and still sent quite a bit of light into the cells.

I also discovered when I tried to lay down in my bunk that if I laid my head on my blanket, as it was wedged between the edge of my "boat" and the side of the immoveable desk, my feet still hung off the lower edge of my bunk. With my arms by my side, I touched both sides of the "boat" at the same time. Although the temperature in the section remained at a constant sixty eight degrees, I didn't need the blanket for cover and I could use it as a pillow. I slept in my orange jumpsuit and pulled the flat sheet up for cover.

And about this cover sheet. I held it up toward the lights and I could count the weave lines, the sheet was so thin. At least it wasn't orange.

Though my anxiety level was still high, I found I was able to doze because I would suddenly awaken from a "bump" sounding from below. I'm still not certain as to how the sound was made, but a drum beat started up and a guy also started "rapping." I couldn't understand the words he was saying but soon he stopped and another voice picked up the rhythm. This continued through several guys and then Charles explained that they were having a "rap-off." This was a contest to see who could continue making up rhymes. I guess the champion was supposed to win some more sugar snacks or something. At any rate, after the soloists finished, one guy started another style of "rap" and then a back-up group joined in. It actually was a lot of fun listening to them, but it certainly wasn't allowing me to get any sleep.

I had again dozed off when about 3:55 A.M. the loudspeaker squawked, "Reynolds. Medical call." I had barely awakened enough to recognize my name was being called when Lars Collins stuck his head around the wall and said they were calling me for a medical check, to go down and stand at the section door. I was somewhat dazed from my short nap, but I staggered down the stairs to the door. It opened and I made my way through to the visitor's area. Shortly, I was instructed by a voice over the loudspeaker to proceed through that section to the medical area. On my way through, I was joined by a couple of other prisoners from other sections, all looking sleep deprived.

When the second door opened, a guard stood about fifty feet away. He ordered all of us to stand where we were until our names were called. He called my name first and I entered the nurse's station. A female nurse proceeded to check my blood pressure, check my blood-sugar count, gave me some of my medicine and then dismissed me. This all took place in probably less than five minutes. As I stood up, I saw a clock on the wall. It read 4:10 A.M. When I returned to my section, one of the prisoners asked me what time it was. I told him it was four ten when I left the nurse's station.

He commented, "Breakfast in about an hour."

I went up the stairs and sat down in my "boat" cross legged, my back to the wall, and contemplated the events of the previous long hours. I prayed. I thanked God for His protection and asked Him to keep His hands on my family. There was still quite a bit of talking and laughing coming from the lower level. It had never ceased throughout the night. However, the upper level appeared to be unusually quiet. I continued to pray until the lights came on, announcing breakfast. It was about 5:15 A.M. on Wednesday and it found me still locked up.

Still wearing orange.

Always orange.

CHAPTER 9

WEDNESDAY, JANUARY 28, 2004 THE ACCUSED

The three most exciting and exhilarating moments that a prisoner has during the normal course of a day are breakfast time, lunch time and supper time. Between those times, a prisoner is left pretty much to his own devises to pass the time. Other than to receive visits from family members and attorneys or visit the medical clinic, there are not many other opportunities to leave the section or cells.

At 11:00 P.M. each night, the television is turned off by the guards, as well as the lights over the cells. The lights over the "Dayroom" stay on 24-7. So when breakfast is announced between five and six o'clock in the morning, it is accompanied by the bright lights being turned on over the cells. Thus, the prisoners are never in total darkness, but the lights coming on announce the beginning of another day.

When the doors opened, a metal rolling carrier stacked with food trays was brought in by a pair of trustees. The food trays were all heavy plastic. Just about all of the prisoners would immediately arise and line up to get a tray with their names on it. Being a diabetic afforded me a special tray with extra food on it. It was specially marked and some of the guys joked about the special treatment I was receiving. As the days passed and other meals were served similarly, I felt fortunate that an attempt was being made to meet my dietary requirements. Except when I first entered the facility, this was being done without me having to say anything at all. At each meal, a specially marked tray with my name on it was given to me.

The special attention seemed to draw more observation from the other prisoners because, if prisoners have any preoccupations, it's food. During my first breakfast, I was surprised to hear the room filled with shouts of "bread for oatmeal," and "eggs for jelly," as well as other sounds of trade and barter. Some of the men saved some of their food for later while many more of the guys ate everything on their trays plus whatever was not eaten by other prisoners.

I took my tray and walked back up the stairs to sit on the edge of my "boat." I had looked around the "Dayroom" for a seat at a table but they were all taken. Phillips and Charles ate at a table on the lower level while Mike Ross sat at the desk in our cell. While there were plenty of breakfast items on my tray and I had not eaten but little since lunch at the Cracker Barrel Restaurant the day before, I was not the least bit hungry. I ate some of the fruit, took a bite of bread and swallowed down the whole half-pint of milk at one time. I set my tray under my knees and continued to sit and watch the activity below.

I started to rise and take my tray below when Mike asked, "If you're not going to eat the rest of that, can I have it? I'll take your tray down for you when I finish."

I told him, "Sure. You can have it." He proceeded to devour all that I had left on the tray.

From that time until I left that cell, Mike would watch me at meal times and would always politely ask if he could have anything that I didn't eat. I always had leftovers because the whole time that I was incarcerated my appetite was minimal. Obviously the emotional strain of being in jail affected my ability to eat. There was a variety of food served and made available, and it was nourishing, but it was always very bland and sometimes tasteless. Although, I must admit that my judgment of the food is limited because I did not eat very much while I was incarcerated. I went into jail weighing 192 and I would come out weighing 181.

Breakfast time lasted until about 6:00 A.M. Many guys lay back down to nap. The television was turned on for the day, but mostly the morning was a quiet time. I had found that a number of books were stacked behind the stairs on the lower level. I picked out a Western novel and read it some, then studied the Bible. At 7:30 A.M. my name was again called over the loudspeaker, and I was ordered to meet a deputy at the section door.

When the section door opened, I was met by a jail guard who identified me. He then ordered me to follow him toward the hall door. We walked through the attorney/client visitor area, past the nurse's station/medical clinic and into the jail office center where I had been held temporarily the previous night. I was told to stand on the same spot where my photograph had been taken. Shortly thereafter, Magistrate Judge Cindy S. Stacey called me to stand before her at the counter. I stepped forward, and she read the charges against me, the amount of the bail, and then I was read my rights. When I acknowledged that I understood the charges, she gave me a copy and instructed me to follow the deputy back to my cell. I had just experienced my "first appearance" and "bond hearing."

About three hours after returning to my cell, I was informed over the loudspeaker that I had a visitor. Again a deputy sheriff met me at the section door as it opened. He escorted me to a small room behind the jail office center, not far from the nurse's station. It was a very small room with one wall consisting of a thick glass partition. A small wooden stool sat in front of the partition with a telephone mounted on the wall. From the other side of the partition, I could see my friend and pastor, Dr. Jerry Patterson coming in.

He and I had met each other thousands of times over the years, through many situations both happy and sad. I don't know if I had ever seen his eyes more doleful and dismal than when he sat down across from me. Though he smiled at my comment concerning my fashionable orange coveralls, the smile didn't reach his eyes. He told me he had not slept the previous night, worrying about me and praying for me. My emotions and feelings were overwhelmed with humbleness that he would care so much. I felt like my head was being hammered by the idea that I was not worth the trouble I was causing this great man. The feeling grew even more as he related how he had tried to use two different properties, in two separate counties, to secure my bond but was rejected in both of them. He told me that he had talked with Alison in Ohio and that she was rushing back to Georgia that afternoon. In the meantime, he suggested I sign a quitclaim to my wife for some property we owned in Rockdale County. I agreed and he promised to return later with a quitclaim for me to sign. He stated that he wasn't positive that any property that I owned could be used for the bond. I told him if necessary we could use some property my sister and I owned together.

THE DOCTOR

When news came to me that Jim had been taken into custody and placed in the Rockdale County Jail, I went to see him as soon as possible. I also obtained what I thought was the necessary information needed to get a bond posted for his release. However, this turned out to be much more difficult than any of us had imagined. There was one setback after another. On my visits to Jim, I would share with him how things were going and his standard reply was, "Well, I know you folks are doing the best you can. It'll finally work out."

And indeed it did.

THE OFFICE MANAGER

The fear was gone but the situation was not. It cycled around and around, becoming worse with each revolution. Interviews at the workplace became recorded phone conversations. Questioning at the police station became more questioning. Being placed in jail became spending the night in jail. Spending days in jail became days without medical prescriptions that remained at home. Finding no evidence of wrongdoing became trying harder to find such evidence. How could such a little "nothing" become such a huge "must be something?"

THE ACCUSED

I was back to waiting again. Throughout the rest of the day and into the evening I spent my time talking with my "posse," reading Scriptures and renewing my proficiency in chess. I'm certainly not a master chessman, but I gained some respect of the other guys by winning a few matches and losing some tightly fought contests. The winner of matches held the table and played the next contestant. Being "new," several challenged me to games, and I was fortunate to hold my own.

Not only were the matches helping me to pass the time, but after each game, the ones watching discussed the various strategies employed by the contestants and either the good moves or the inexperienced errors that occurred. At any rate, I didn't add anyone else to my "posse." Through these conversations, I made acquaintances that would help me to avoid any later problems when my true case was exposed. Up until then, the actual nature of the charges against me was not known by any of the other prisoners. I was attempting to do everything that I could to keep it that way. The stories I had heard in the past about how anyone accused of any involvement with children were made into open game by other prisoners made me wary that someone would want to build their reputation at my expense. I didn't think that pleas of innocence would be very effective in stopping anyone who wanted to harm me. Thus far, I had not received any insinuations that anyone suspected what the charges were against me, though I did feel that my vague answers to such inquiries concerning my case were raising suspicions.

Later, as Charles and I were talking with each other, he made the comment that he thought I had seemed to assimilate myself much better with the prisoners than he had. He said he "hated" being in jail and was just enduring his time. He declared he was not of the same "mindset" as many of the other guys and he was refusing to allow himself to get the "jailhouse mentality." He told me that some of the guys, including the others in our cell, had been in and out of jail so many times that the "jailhouse mentality" was fully developed and that they did not know how to exist outside of a jailhouse environment. He insisted that he wasn't going to allow that to happen to him, and he observed that he felt the same toward me; I wasn't of the "jailhouse mentality" either. I told him I had never been in jail before in my life and that I had a lot of fear in me. By assimilating, I was simply trying to blend in and make friends so as to survive. Though I'm sure my language may have appeared unusually forthright and forceful, Charles consoled me by telling me that he thought I had "adjusted" very quickly and was handling everything well. He said he overheard several of the guys saying that I didn't appear to deserve being in jail.

Charles said that since he was locked up two weeks before, he had not gone into the "Dayroom" except to get his meals. He hadn't played chess or checkers and had not attempted to befriend any of the guys outside of our cell. I told him I'd be happy to play a game of chess with him if he wanted and he readily agreed. When we had our match later on that evening, we found ourselves very evenly matched with our skill levels corresponding. He won most of the matches but not without difficulty. I may not have been a champion player and not given him very much competition, but overall it was helping me to survive and keeping my mind off of my horrible situation.

At some point during the afternoon, I was called back to the visitor's area. When I arrived, a female Deputy Sheriff was waiting with a paper for me to sign. She explained that Dr. Patterson had brought a quitclaim, releasing my title to land that Alison and I had owned jointly. He was going to attempt to use it to secure my bond. Another Deputy with her witnessed my signature and she notarized the document. She told me she would return the paper to Dr. Patterson, who was waiting outside.

Wednesday evenings are reserved for religious services for those who wish to attend. The service is held in a "meeting room" located off of the central circular hallway. These services probably provide the only opportunity for prisoners from other sections to mix with each other. On this particular evening about twenty guys from Section "C" joined about fifteen men from Section "D" for a Bible study.

A young man dressed in blue jeans and a khaki shirt met us in the "meeting room," greeting each prisoner with a handshake and a hug. He had visited there many times in the past and knew several of the prisoners by name. After prayer, he spoke for about an hour, telling of his own time in jail and how Christ had turned his life around. He spoke in the lingo of the "street" and was very earnest and sincere in what he had to say. When he asked for commitments, eight of the prisoners went up to pray. Overall, it was an encouraging experience and uplifting service; I was happy to see some of the prisoners take steps to begin changing their lives. Afterwards, my "posse" and I had a great discussion concerning the Scriptures and expanding our spiritual knowledge and acceptance. I shared my Holy Ghost experience with them and all four stated they were tired of making poor choices and desired a chance to make better ones.

As evening and "lights out" time approached, I was thankful for God's protection, and I was grateful for Dr. Patterson and my family and for all they were doing in attempting to secure my bond. I was still anxious over my situation. Being in a room with thirty or more men who might become dangerous if my true case became known held no comfort for me.

I had continued to cement my relationship with my "posse" throughout the day by giving away most of my meals. I still wasn't hungry at lunch time, which meant I shared my sandwiches with Mike and Lars. Then the evening meal came and Mike got most of it, sharing with the other guys. They all got a bonus when about 10:30 P.M. a Deputy Sheriff came to the door of our section and called my name. He said the institutional dietician had ordered that I receive a late-night snack as part of my diabetic diet. He handed me a sack filled with two peanut butter and jelly sandwiches and an apple. Several of the guys hooted and hollered at me for being treated "special," but I just smiled and waved my hand at them. I went back to my upper level cell where my "posse" was sitting and told them they could split up my sandwiches. All I wanted was the apple. You would have thought I was Santa Claus the way they reacted when I gave them the sandwiches. It was a unique situation for them to have a late-night snack and they wanted to know if I was going to continue to receive it while I was there. I told them I guessed so and that was a side benefit for being my "posse." For the first time, I called them by that name and they gave a hearty laugh all the way around. They said they thought being called my "posse" was pretty cool. Especially if I continued to not have much of an appetite!

As I settled down to nap for a while, before medical call would again be made at four o'clock in the morning, little did I realize that the media had gotten possession of my story and picture and were about to broadcast their explosive news to the whole world.

CHAPTER 10

THURSDAY, JANUARY 29, 2004 THE ACCUSED

The day began as the previous day, as I went for a medical check at the nurse's station and returned to my cell restlessly to wait for breakfast. Afterwards, despite feeling the physical deprivation from the lack of sleep, I was unable to even take a nap. I simply read Scriptures while most of the other prisoners slept or talked together in low voices. At about 9:00 A.M. I was told over the loudspeaker that I had a visitor. I made my way to the "telephone booth" room and there sat Dr. Jerry Patterson waiting for me.

When I picked up the phone to speak to Dr. Patterson, I told him that I was sorry I could not keep our usual Thursday morning breakfast appointment. For quite some time, he and I had met on Thursday

143

mornings as long-time friends and enjoyed a casual time of fellowship and conversation, as only two old friends can enjoy. He said under the circumstances he understood but that we would have to restart as soon as I got out. The next thing Dr. Patterson told me was that my wife had returned from Ohio the previous evening. I felt thankful knowing she was again near and hoped the trip had not proven too arduous for her. He then said that the Rockdale Sheriffs Department would not accept the property that Alison and I owned for my bond. Apparently, signing the quit-claim the day before had been a waste of time. As he and I had discussed previously, he was going to contact my sister, Beverly Martin, and arrange for me to sign a quitclaim on property she and I owned jointly in Oglethorpe County, Georgia. He said that he would be able to return with the paperwork for me to sign that day.

He then revealed news that sent shockwaves rampaging through my mind. To say the least, I became perturbed and agitated when he said that my arrest had made the front page of the *Rockdale Citizen* accompanied by my arrest photo. He said the story had also been on several of the Atlanta area radio stations. I felt myself going from dumb-founded to a soul-searing shock at the turn of events. Dr. Patterson expressed his regrets that the news-papers and radio stations were sensationalizing my situation. He felt the best thing we could do was to expedite my release, then go from there. He left me promising to return very soon with the new quitclaim for me to sign.

Located in each section was one telephone mounted on the wall underneath the television. A prisoner was allowed to make collect telephone calls only. Immediately upon returning to my section, I telephoned Alison collect. Alison answered, and it was a tremendous relief to hear her loving voice. She asked several times about my health and how was I feeling and assured me that they were doing all that they could to secure my release. Someone had informed her about the story appearing in the paper, but she said she wasn't interested in reading it. She said that she had been told that the charges concerning a child porno website had been included in the article. We discussed the plans for my release, and I told her that I would call back with any new developments.

THE DOCTOR

I think one of the most difficult things Alison faced was the fact that there were so many unanswered questions in exactly how this situation came to be, as well as the fallout of humiliation and embarrassment that came to them through the media. The media reporting seemed to be partial toward guilt and produced and presented Jim in the worse possible light. Alison was frustrated that those whom she loved so deeply were hurt and she was helpless. Even though she was deeply hurt herself by all that was happening, she never focused only on her pain, except as it was helpful in getting the whole family through this ordeal.

THE ACCUSED

I went to my bunk on the upper level, worried sick that the news of the charges against me was going to be revealed to the other prisoners. I was literally afraid at what might happen. I had not been settled down for more than thirty minutes when, about 10:50 A.M., my name was again called out over the loudspeaker, and I was ordered to report to the visitor's area. Again, I was met by the same female Deputy Sheriff with another quitclaim for me to sign. This time she did not have another Deputy with her to witness my signature. Just at that moment, a male prisoner who was being transferred to another section stepped through the doorway behind me. She ordered him to stop, stand right there beside me and watch me sign my name. I signed my name and she turned to the prisoner and asked, "Did you see him sign that paper?"

The prisoner replied, "Yes," at which point she pointed at a place on the document and told him, "Sign right here. That says you witnessed him signing this deed."

As soon as the prisoner finished signing his name, the Deputy told him to, "Move along now." I returned to my section, sat down in my "boat," lowered my head and began praying that I would be released before the news of the charges against me got out among the prisoner population. I prayed that if I weren't released in time, the Lord would provide protection. Nevertheless, I prayed, "Not my will, but Thine be done."

THE SISTER

On Thursday, January 29, 2004, at 8:20 A.M., my husband, Carl, and I received a telephone call from Dr. Jerry Patterson, Jim's pastor and long time family friend. He told us that Jim had been arrested and jailed on Tuesday afternoon, January 27th. When the call came in, I was on the treadmill doing my daily exercise and not in the house until several minutes after his notification.

When I came in, Carl said that I needed to sit down, that he had something to tell me. I immediately asked if Mother had called because her brother, Delma, was ill with cancer and had been very sick. He said, "No," but that Dr. Patterson had called and told him the disturbing news of Jim's arrest. I lost my breath, my heart racing as if it would jump out of my body. I started shaking all over with fear for my brother, for his health, and for his safety in jail. I did not cry, which is unusual, because I'm very emotional. Dr. Patterson said our mother had not been told, so, we knew immediately that that was our duty and obligation.

Our Mother, Lorene Reynolds, is 84 years old, a widow, and not in very good health, so I was anxious in that regard.

I wanted our sons to go with us because Mother is close to them, and I needed their support as well. Our eldest, Chuck, was unable to go, but our other son, Scott, was available. Scott had become a strong Christian in the last several years and was a man of good faith and belief. He was such a help to us when we talked with Mother at around 9:15 in the morning, and he continued to support Mother, Jim and I throughout the ordeal. Mother did not show a lot of outward emotion at the time we told her of Jim's arrest, but that all came later. I'm sure, like the rest of us, she was quaking on the inside.

Dr. Patterson had related to Carl the amount of the bond and his attempts to raise the bond on his own. We were told that a property (real estate) bond was acceptable, so we decided to use Mother's house as bond since it was already in both mine and Jim's name. It had been that way since 1995.

Around 10:30 A.M. we found out that Jim's name would have to come off the deed and that he would have to sign it over to me. We had discussed the previous year that I would buy his share in the future. Carl and I were ready to drive to Conyers to post bond, but after the telephone call telling us that his name needed to be taken off the deed, I went to the local library and faxed the property information to Jim's office. Dr. Patterson was going to carry that information, along with some other forms to the jail for Jim's signature, then bring them to us to have the deed recorded at the Oglethorpe County Courthouse in Lexington before it closed at 5:00 P.M.

We met Dr. Patterson at the Oglethorpe County Courthouse around 2:30 P.M. (He had waited at Jim's office for our property information, taken it immediately to the jail for Jim's signature and driven directly to meet us.) We were able to file the quitclaim and have it recorded. At approximately 3:00 P.M. we went to the Oglethorpe County Sheriffs Office to get the necessary papers that would be posted for bond. There we ran into the proverbial brick wall. The Sheriff was in Atlanta investigating a case and the people left "in charge" were rude, obnoxious, unhelpful and unrelenting in every way possible.

First, we were told that Oglethorpe County could not post bond for another county, which we later determined to be completely false. Then we were informed that the value of the property had to be three times the bond, which is not true in all other counties. Jim's bond was $60,000, which meant the property had to be worth $180,000 according to their contention! They said that other counties required even more than Oglethorpe County to handle an out-of-county bond. (We later contacted our attorney, Suzanne Burton, who also serves as a Judge in neighboring Clarke County, and she verified that Clarke County only charges $25 to expedite bonds for other counties.) We were then told that only the Oglethorpe County Sheriff could approve dollar for dollar bail and that they did not know when he would return. After numerous unsuccessful calls were made by Carl, it was apparent we could not get in touch with the Sheriff. The Sheriff's Office staff was not helpful in regard to contacting the Sheriff either, although they did have access to him in case of an emergency.

We left a request for the Sheriff to call us. He never did. Jim's attorney, Gary Moore, and the Rockdale County Sheriffs Department tried to get the Oglethorpe County Sheriff to return their calls after Dr. Patterson had called them and advised them of the problems we were running into, but to no avail. We called people we knew, who also knew the Sheriff to try and contact him, but no one could reach him. Additionally, there was no one in his office who had the authority to sign off on the necessary papers we needed.

We went back to Mother's house about 4:30 P.M. and for the next hour and a half, Carl and Dr. Patterson were still making calls and trying everything possible. At one point we were coming up with a cash bond of $9,200, but if we posted cash, we were advised, it would be gone forever. Jim's attorney wanted the property bond, if at all possible, and felt that would be the best way to go.

THE ACCUSED

I felt afraid. My stomach was twisted into knots. I wanted to weep, cry out loud, bang my fists on the walls, and yell to the top of my lungs, all at the same time. I felt more nervous than I had ever felt in my life. I could see that my hands were visibly shaking. I knew if I tried to speak to anyone, there would be a noticeable quiver to my voice. The tenseness in my neck and shoulders was almost unbearable. At the same time, I felt an overwhelming concern for Alison and my family and for what they may be going through. I didn't think I could be much help to any of them, but I decided to call Alison again to find out if anything else was going on. Unfortunately, there was.

I called Alison collect just before noon and told her about signing the quitclaim on the Oglethorpe County property. I hoped this would finally work out my bond. Alison then told me that the situation around our house had become almost unbearable. She said that a mobile television crew from WSB-TV had parked in front of our house. She related to me that a newsman had attempted to interview my office staff as they walked to the "cottage," but that they had refused to talk with him. She said it looked like he also may have been trying to interview some of our neighbors. She told me that she hadn't been outside and she was not going to leave the house until they left.

It seemed my dismay and agitation escalated to a new level. Over my head and throughout the jail, televisions were playing. The noon-time news, the five o'clock news and the six o'clock news were all going to be playing. If my story hit, I felt I would be in mortal danger. I didn't relay any of this to Alison because she was dealing with enough as it was. I hung up the telephone, telling her that I would call her if I found out about any movement toward my release.

THE NEIGHBOR

When I came home from work in the afternoon that day and as I drove toward my home, I saw several people going in and out of our neighbor's house where Jim and Alison Reynolds lived. When I entered my house, my son, Adam, said there had been numerous people at Jim's house when he had come home from school. I went into my bedroom when the front doorbell rang and Adam answered the door. He called to me and I went to the door, finding a reporter from WSB-TV Channel 2 standing there, holding a microphone. I wondered what in the world was going on.

THE ACCUSED

I went back to my bunk, surrendering myself to prayer. My "posse" seemed to realize I was troubled, but they were kind enough, at that point, to allow me to be alone—as much alone as you can be with forty other guys running around. As the noon hour approached, I fervently prayed that the news of my arrest would not be broadcast in my section. Each day, one prisoner is in charge of changing the channels. Fortunately, whosever day it was, he decided not to have it on WSB-TV. I do not remember what channel was on, but it did not carry the story of my arrest. I thanked God for His protection, and I prayed my bond would come through very quickly.

Little did I know that during that very same hour, CNN was carrying the story of my arrest, broadcasting the story around the world. Rev. Guy Garner and his family had known me for a score of years and they were working in Israel when they saw the story of my arrest on CNN. They called Dr. Patterson wanting to know what was going on. They told him to tell me that their prayers would be for my safe deliverance.

Unbelievably, the story of my arrest was going around the world.

THE NEIGHBOR

The television reporter asked me if I was aware of what was going on next door. I told him, "No," but I had noticed the activity. He then went on to explain that Jim had been arrested on child pornography charges. He asked me what I thought. I told him I did not believe it was true for a minute. There had to be some explanation. He also asked if I knew his wife had left. I again said I did not know about that.

THE ACCUSED

The five o'clock and six o'clock news came and went, and again the story of my arrest did not appear. I had prayed during that whole time that God would protect me and He answered my prayer, in that the station being watched in my section was not WSB-TV. However, later I was to learn that the story had been shown on most of the other televisions throughout the jail. Thankfully, it wasn't shown in my section, but it became evident that the guards were not as quick to turn off the televisions in the other sections. In some instances, the televisions remained on throughout the broadcast and were seen by many of the prisoners.

THE NEIGHBOR

We watched the early evening newscast; shocked at the manner this story was being handled. They played the part of my interview with the reporter where I defended Jim. Surprisingly, Monica Kaufman, one of the news anchors, made the comment at the end of the story that it must be remembered that the accused is to be considered innocent until proven guilty. We had never heard her nor any other broadcaster state such an opinion before or since.

Later that evening my husband, Ed, and I went over to Jim's house to see Alison. Alison said that she was doing well and that there had been a lot of support from those who knew Jim. Ed and I were concerned for Alison's safety as the television newscast had shown the address and the street name of their house. We both felt this was totally irresponsible on the TV station's part. We told her we would be watching out for her. I think that my husband being a policeman was reassuring to Alison.

It was horrible to think that Jim had to spend the night in jail while another neighbor, Gary Moore, worked to get him released. I remember thinking how quick the media was there to report his arrest and I wondered if they would be there as fast when he was exonerated. Jim's attorney, Gary, even mentioned the same thing when he was interviewed by the media.

THE FRIEND

On a cold January night, I was told of something too awful to believe. My friend, Jimmy Reynolds, whom I have known for forty plus years, had been arrested and charged with operating a child porno website. That night on the news I heard what I thought had to be a terrible mistake. *NO WAY,* was my first thought. I had known Jimmy since childhood. We had attended youth camps together, attended church together, worked on church plays together, and I had even worked for him at times. My family had visited and stayed in his home on many occasions. I knew this was just not right.

As soon as my children heard the news, they were on the phone calling to see if I had heard from Jimmy or his family. They did not believe any of the accusations for even a minute. My daughter, Lynn, told me, "Daddy, there is no way this could be true. Out of all the times I stayed at his house growing up, I would have seen or felt something was wrong. But I never for one moment experienced anything out of place. He was always a gentleman and very careful to always knock before he entered our room or his daughter's room."

My son, Keith, told me he did not know what he would have done growing up if Jimmy had not been there. Keith would turn to him for advice when he couldn't come to me. Jimmy had always treated my family as his own. My wife and I knew that this was all just plain crazy and we felt it was so unfair for this to be happening to such a good family.

Jimmy's mother and father were like my own. His father, Enoch (everyone called him 'Sarge'), and I went fishing many times together. Sarge was the kindest and most gentle man I had ever known. In my opinion, Jimmy had always had a lot of his father's character in him. And his mother, Lorene, was a sweetheart. But you talk about grit and gumption; she was eighty-five pounds of pure stubbornness. Jimmy got a lot of that trait also. I hope that combination gave Jimmy all he needed to survive this ordeal.

Jimmy's family and my family attended church together in Athens, Georgia, pastored by my brother, Dr. Jerry A. Patterson. Jimmy was trusted with children of all ages while serving as Sunday School Superintendent, Youth Minister and directing many church programs and plays. Those children, now adults, would stand up for his credibility even to this day.

When my brother moved to Conyers, Georgia, to begin a new church in 1981, Jimmy and his family also moved and continued to work with young people in various ways. One position he held for a number of years was in the leadership of our Boy Scout Troop. He was always ready to help anyone with anything that he could.

THE CHAIRMAN

It has been my honor to have known Jim Reynolds for at least ten years, working and interacting with him on many, various levels, most recently in my capacity as Chairman of the Wise Men Give Him Gifts Funding Committee for Faith Tabernacle Church. Over these years, there have been many occasions where I have conferred with him, discussed with him, "brain-stormed" with him, laughed and cried with him and worshipped with him. Together we have been involved in several business deals, both good and bad. I have seen this man in very good times in his life and in one of the darkest times of his life. Throughout, he was always the same. As Shakespeare is reported to have written, "Consistency, thou art a jewel."

When Jim was arrested for the charges alleged against him, I knew there was no way this man was guilty. I felt sadness and hurt for him and his family.

When a local television reporter attempted to make the case against Jim salacious and ugly by focusing on Jim's involvement in a Pentecostal church (the words this reporter used were "… high up in the Pentecostal church."). I became angry, and my righteous indignation was kindled. It was very obvious that this reporter thought he had latched onto another "Elmer Gantry" or Jimmy Swaggart story which would resound from the halls of many Pentecostal churches as Jim Reynolds was "shown" to be a trafficker in child pornography.

THE SISTER

Finally, about 6:00 P.M., we knew that the Oglethorpe County Sheriff was not going to return our call or okay the bond. So, reluctantly, we left

Mother's house with sadness and a heavy heart, knowing that Jim would be in jail another night.

As night time came, my imagination worked overtime as to how Jim was being treated by the guards and by his cellmates, wondering if he was able to get his medication and what kind of food he was being given. I was very anxious about his health, safety and his emotional well being. In my imagination, he was curled up tightly on his cot and filled with fear. My heart was breaking. I sat up all night, dozing occasionally in my chair.

THE ACCUSED

Supper time and the early evening news time passed, and I resigned myself to having to spend another night in jail. Apparently my bond was meeting legal roadblocks again and my bail was being prevented. I decided to involve myself in more chess matches in hopes of relieving the anxiety and stress I was feeling, now fearing the newscasts that would start at 10:00 P.M. Thankfully the television in my section was not tuned to a station that broadcasted a ten o'clock news program. It was later tuned to WSB-TV. Their newscast was scheduled for 11:00 P.M.

Sitting at a table in the "Dayroom" with the television blaring overhead, playing a game of chess with Charles, I was concentrating with a great deal of difficulty when some one hollered, "Whoo-whooo." Another laughed and said very loudly, "Look up there!" I did not turn my head toward the television in fear of what I would see, but someone else cried out, "Hey, James. Look. There you are." Someone else picked up the cadence and said, "There you are, man." By the time I did turn my head to look toward the television, the advertisement for the eleven o'clock news on WSB-TV had moved to other "exciting stories coming up." I ducked my head back down, saying not a word to anyone, pretending to concentrate on my chess game. Shortly thereafter, another ad appeared touting the upcoming news broadcast featuring "The arrest of a Conyers businessman on child pornography charges." This time when I looked up, I caught a glimpse of my arrest picture on the screen. Someone unseen called out, "Hey. We got us a celebrity in here." I overheard another prisoner say, "I didn't know we had someone famous in here with us." A large prisoner I had not spoken with before tapped me on the shoulder and asked, "How does it feel to be famous?" and turned to walk off, laughing what I would consider a very sinister laugh.

I continued to sit at the table with Charles and Lars Collins sitting next to me. Phillips and Mike Ross were sitting at a table just behind me. They had obviously seen the television ad, heard the catcalls and could probably tell I was becoming very nervous. Charles motioned with his finger for me to lean toward him. As I did, Lars also leaned over.

"Don't worry. No one is going to bother you. It'll be alright. We're watching."

I told him that I would tell them the whole story later.

Fortunately, the guards turned the television off early that evening, before the news program was broadcasted. The guys in my section had only seen the news promotional spots and not the full newscast. That was not the case throughout the remainder of the jail. The guards allowed the televisions to remain on past the eleven o'clock news in some sections and those prisoners were afforded the full story, as depicted by the media.

No one in my section said anything else, nor was I confronted as I made my way to the upper level to my "boat." Charles and Lars walked one in front of me and another behind me without my saying a word to them. Phillips and Mike followed about three minutes later. I tried to walk up the stairs without making eye contact with anyone. As I ascended the first steps, I saw a fairly large prisoner lying on a bunk directly behind the stairway, staring at me with a very unfriendly and sinister look. Averting my eyes, I simply kept walking up the stairs.

I had seen and read many stories throughout my life concerning the assaults and even murders of men in prison, who had either been indicted or convicted of crimes involving child molestation, child cruelty or child pornography. Some stories told of how it was almost a cult among prisoners to kill anyone accused or convicted of any crimes against children. Other stories told of how it became a badge of honor among prisoners for one of them to get rid of men accused of a crime against a child. My fear was not unfounded. My trepidation was real. I did not know if I could convince anyone that I was innocent of the charges. Probably every prisoner who was charged with such crimes declared his innocence, right up until the moment he was struck dead. I felt it was entirely possible that some of those accused were also innocent of the charges.

Charles, Lars, Mike and Phillips all sat down around me as I assumed my favorite position in my "boat"—my back to the wall with my legs crossed in front of me. My hands were visibly shaking as I confessed, "Fellows, I am really afraid."

Charles asked me to explain how I came to be locked up. I explained to them that I had been arrested for images that had been found on my computers and that I was being held responsible for those images because they depicted children in sexual activity. I explained further that there was evidence that my identity had been stolen and that someone had created a child porn website using my name. I also told them that there was not any evidence that I had ever bought, traded, solicited or requested any type of child pornography. However, the whole situation boiled down to the fact that images were found on my computers and I was being held responsible for them.

They listened to me attentively and silently throughout my discourse, without any accusatory looks. When I finished my explanation, Charles motioned to the other three to follow him beyond my bunk a little ways where they huddled in intense conversation. I saw them nod their heads in unison as they came back to sit around me, and Charles said, "We have only one question to ask you. Did you in any way, under any circumstances ever touch a child or have you ever been sexually involved with a child?"

I looked at him and the others and said, "No, absolutely not. The charges are for possession of pictures, but, at any rate, no. I've not been involved with any children in any manner. Not physically. Not by telephone. Not by e-mails. Not in a chat room. Nothing like that at all."

Obviously the truthfulness of my statements was sensed and my sincerity was detected for they turned to each other and nodded their heads. Charles told me that they had decided that they would watch out for me and that they would help me if there was any trouble. He stated, "We've got your back."

Mike and Phillips patted me on my back and said "okay" and "it's going to be alright." My emotions were full at this display of friendship among four guys I had not known previously. I told them, "Thank you," and told them that my "posse" would have a special place in my prayers. They laughed and Mike said, "Posses are supposed to go out and catch bad guys. I guess we're supposed to protect the good guys!"

They continued to banter about being a "posse" and apparently took pride in the designation. I stood and we talked while leaning against the bunk, although I remained reticent and reserved. Apparently my quiet demeanor alarmed Lars for he stared at me and then surprised me when he asked, "You're not going to hurt yourself, are you?"

Admittedly I was distraught at my situation overall, but the thought of committing suicide had not crossed my mind. I still answered with, "No, I don't think so," and my four friends said, "Sit down," and began talking with me. Lars related stories of men who had become so disturbed at their circumstances that they killed themselves and he did not want to see me get that distressed. He and the other three started talking to me in soft voices, utilizing Scriptures to encourage me and to calm my fears. Phillips went to his bunk and pulled out a notebook and began sharing poetry that he had written. His material was very good, although I can't recall any of his rhymes. However, from that day on he became known as "The Poet."

When the lights were turned off, except for those in the "Dayroom," and the guys started settling down for the evening, Lars retired to his cell. Charles, Mike and "The Poet" continued talking with me as each lay in his bunk. I can't remember all of the things that were discussed, but I do remember at one point, again expressing my fear that someone in our section would become angry over the charges against me and would attempt to harm me. Almost as one, they all expressed that they believed in me and that they wouldn't let anyone bother me. The expression that I remember being used the most by them is the one that kept me calm, "Don't worry. We've got your back."

I don't know if those four guys, my "posse," realized it or not but God used them to probably save my life and to help me from losing my sanity that night.

Their words, "we've got your back," at least helped me not to feel like I was facing this situation alone. I believe God spoke through them to let me know that Someone was watching over me and was on my side.

Despite the encouraging words and the comfort my "posse" attempted to give me, I remained cautious and afraid. Every once in a while, I looked over at Mike and "The Poet" and throughout that whole night, one of them was awake. Sometimes they would speak to me, other times I would just catch a glimpse of their eyes glancing over to where I was laying. Intentionally or not, I felt they were watching over me. However, I still jumped every time someone coughed, moved or got up during the night.

Early on I thought about what I would do if I was confronted by someone that I thought wanted to harm me. The only thing I could come up with was the fact that I was about four feet from the heavy steel door that separated our section from the solitary confinement cell. I calculated approximately how much time it would take for me to stand up from my "boat," take the four steps to get inside that area and push the steel door closed. It appeared that the only way that door could be opened, after it was pushed closed, was with a key. I realized that my only defense would be to get into that room and shut the door until the guards could come and release me.

Until I had to actually do something like that, I knew that my best protection was the Lord. So I prayed throughout the night, and though I felt unworthy to ask for His protection, I still prayed earnestly and asked God to cover me with Wings of Mercy. The night passed without an incident. I did not hear any other catcalls or negative comments from anyone. In fact, an unexpected sense of peace descended over me and permeated throughout my section as another day began.

THE FRIEND

By the time I heard about Jimmy, he was already in jail. I could not talk with him or see him. I could not even imagine the hell he must have been going through. This was a Godly man and, during his lifetime, his only encounters with the law had been a couple of speeding tickets. He was not a man with a "rap sheet." For this man to be in jail would be like putting your ten-year old son in prison. Being inside a jail with all of the bad elements that already fill our jail cells and prisons, locked behind bars with men you do not know anything about and who had done only God knows what, the thought of being afraid to even close your eyes to go to sleep, or even afraid to move around at all, must have been pure torture for him. I could not comprehend what it must have been like to go through what he was going through.

CHAPTER 11

FRIDAY,
JANUARY 30, 2004
THE ACCUSED

At approximately 4:00 A.M. on this Friday morning, my name was called over the loudspeaker and I was ordered to report to the medical clinic. My mind felt dull from the lack of sleep and the lack of food, not that there had not been plenty available, but I simply did not have an appetite. My orange flip-flops click-clacked as I made my way through the sliding door and quietly moved into the circular hallway. During my other visits to the nurse's station, I had been accompanied by only a couple of other prisoners joining me from the other sections. I became instantly alert as I heard several of the section doors open and close. I soon sensed that during this trip I would be accompanied by seven others, and only one of them did I recognize from previous trips to the clinic.

My dullness of mind disappeared instantly as I wondered if any of these guys recognized me from the news broadcasts. I nervously looked at each one of them, but they all appeared to be dazed and simply wanting to get this visit over with so they could return to their bunks. Blessedly, I was the first one called and my visit was uneventful. I returned toward my section door without making eye contact with any other of the prisoners standing in line for the nurse's station. It was unsettling to walk the hallway without seeing a guard in sight, and I was almost eager to rejoin my "posse."

Breakfast was served early that morning, about forty-five minutes after I returned to my section. In fifteen minutes, all of my fellow inmates in Section "C" were either back in bed or walking around talking in quiet voices. I again gave away most of my food to my "posse" and I then went to the bathroom facilities to wash off and brush my teeth. When I finished, I started back to my open cell but stopped at the railing overlooking the "Dayroom." I placed one foot on the bottom railing and leaned my arms over the top metal bar. I stood that way for several minutes, alone. I observed the activity below as the usual normal morning bustle began that I had become accustomed to over the past three days. Regardless, there was an unusual quietness in both the upper and lower levels. I actually marveled at the peacefulness and quiet. There was not the usual loud talking and laughing banter of previous mornings. I had been anticipating a confrontation from some of the guys concerning the charges against me, but instead I began to feel a calmness and peacefulness of mind and spirit, totally unexpected. I actually shook my head when I realized that I was not nervous anymore. My stomach wasn't queasy, and I didn't feel the shaking inside of my body. My fear had dissipated with the night. I felt a divine serenity and reflected on David's words, "Thou preparest a table before me in the presence of mine enemies..." (Psalm 23:5).

I believe that somehow, through God's grace and mercy, His Spirit and the Angels, a supernatural calmness and peace had descended into Section "C" and all of my fears and dread had faded away like mists in the sunlight.

"Posse" member Lars Collins came over, accompanied by a couple of other guys that were new to our section. We introduced ourselves to each other and then Lars quietly asked me if I was doing all right. I told him, "Yes," and he said that he had been worried about me and had prayed for me. He said he was still concerned that I would hurt myself, but I assured him I was okay and felt fine. I still had not given any contemplation to injuring myself, but I understood that my look of distress the previous evening may have appeared to them as if I would resort to suicide. Instead, I had resorted to the Rock of Ages and It had cleft for me, a much better option.

We stood there for a few minutes discussing a hobby of one of the new guys, World War II aircraft. After a short conversation, I excused myself and went back to my "boat" and sat down. I picked up my Bible and began to read. Charles, Mike and "The Poet" were lying down in our cell. Lars had walked back to his cell next to mine and was sitting and talking with the new guys. I sat there for about fifteen minutes when suddenly the quiet was interrupted by the sounds of our section door opening.

Breakfast had already been served, and it was certainly too early for lunch to be brought in, so the clanging of the door was a mystery. Everything became absolutely silent except for the sound of the door sliding open. Normally when the doors were opened, it was preceded by an announcement over the loudspeaker or a call for one of the prisoners. The door opening now, without any warning, was very startling because it was totally unexpected. I had no idea what was happening nor why and I sat in my bunk staring at the opening door.

As soon as there was room for a person to squeeze by the opening door, an armed Swat-team member wearing full riot gear came in and positioned himself in the center of the "Dayroom." Another guard dressed the same as the first one entered and stationed himself beside the open door. Behind him entered two more, similarly dressed, and they marched directly towards the stairway leading to the upper level. I watched from my sitting position in my bunk as one guard stopped at the foot of the stairs and faced toward the center of the "Dayroom," swiveling his head from side to side. The last guard climbed the stairs. It was apparent to me something serious was going on, but as to what I could not even begin to contemplate.

The section was eerily silent as the guard climbed the stairs, his studded boots ringing loudly off of the metal steps. What little talking and commotion had been going on ceased immediately! The only thought that finally crossed my mind was that the guards were there to take away the prisoner from the solitary cell that had been placed there the previous day. Or maybe they were there to transfer all of us to another area. I just continued to sit cross legged on my bunk with my Bible in my lap and watched them.

The fourth officer reached the head of the stairs and stood directly next to the foot of my "boat." He stopped suddenly, looked down at me, and asked, "You're Reynolds?"

"Yes, sir," I replied.

"Get all of your stuff and come with me," he ordered, looking cautiously around at all of the other prisoners staring at me and him.

I stood and picked up some books Charles had lent me to read and placed them on the desk. Charles had continued to lie on his bunk with his arm across his eyes, unconscious to the activity around him. Turning toward him, I shook his arm and said, "Hey. Charles. I'm putting your books on the desk. It appears I'm leaving."

He rose, blinking his eyes open, and asked, "What's happening?" By this time, the rest of my "posse" were rising and wondering what was going on too.

Before I could answer, the officer interrupted by saying, "No talking. Let's get moving," still moving his eyes around guardedly.

I turned and grabbed the corners of my sheet and made a sack out of it. I placed all of my things in the middle of it and threw it over my shoulder like a tote bag. The officer asked me if that was everything, and I told him it was. He then instructed me to precede him down the stairs. As I reached the top step, I turned to my "posse," my guardian angels, and tossed my hand up in a wave of goodbye. I said, "See ya'll later." Unfortunately, I've never seen any of them since.

When I reached the foot of the stairs, the officer waiting there walked in front of me through the doorway. The officer behind me instructed another prisoner to grab my "boat" and take it to the hallway, where he left it. After we walked into the hallway, the two other officers exited the section and the door slid closed behind them. When they reached the hallway, one of the officers instructed me to stand beside a wall while the guards gathered around me and began talking on their shoulder microphones. Two of the guards stood at attention right beside me, one on each side.

We stood there for about five minutes and I decided I would risk asking a question. Until that point, no explanation had been given as to what was going on. I turned to one of the guards standing next to me and in a low voice asked, "Can I ask you where you're taking me and what's going on?"

He hesitated for a second then said, "We're taking you to solitary confinement." My eyebrows rose up at his statement, and seeing the questioning look on my face, he continued, "Some prisoners in other sections saw your face on the television last night and we overheard them making death threats. We are moving you for your own protection."

My heart felt like it had skipped a beat as his words shook me to my soul, but I bowed my head right there and said, "Thank You, Lord, for Your protection." Even in the midst of threats and danger our Lord is more than able to provide protection and to preserve us.

THE FRIEND

Whenever I read an article or heard something on the news about Jimmy, I would get madder and madder. Some of Jimmy's so-called friends and associates completely turned their backs on him, and this when he needed them the most. It was hard for me to understand how they could even doubt this man of such integrity.

THE ACCUSED

We moved through the visitor's area and past the jail offices to the solitary confinement section. I entered into a barred area that was the "Dayroom" for three cells. At one end of the "Dayroom" was an open shower for all of the inmates in those three cells. The "Dayroom" also housed a television that served the three cells. Each cell was eight feet by ten feet and was made to hold two people. None of the cells had windows. A steel bunk bed lined one wall, while the opposite wall held a steel desk and a stainless steel toilet. None of the cells were open cells. Two of the cells had steel mesh doors which opened into the "Dayroom." One cell had a solid metal door with only a small opening in it.

The first cell to my left was the one with the solid door, and I later learned that it held an inmate who was mentally deranged. I could hear yells and grunts coming from beyond the solid steel door. The cell to the far right held two men, while the cell in the middle held one prisoner. When we first entered the solitary confinement area, the guard approached the cell with the solid steel door and opened it. I admit the thought of being confined with this man, who apparently had mental difficulties from the noises he was making, was disconcerting to me. I didn't really want to go in there, and I became concerned that that was what the guard was going to do. The thoughts of being in such a closed-in area without daylight or without being able to see out made me feel claustrophobic. Thankfully the guard hesitated, closed the door, and turned to the young prisoner in the center cell and asked him if he would mind having some company. The prisoner said, "No. I don't mind," and explained that he had been in there alone for ten days.

I said a quiet, "Thank You, Lord."

I had brought my "boat" with me, and the guard instructed me to lean it against a wall in the "Dayroom." The young man in the center cell had been sleeping on the bottom bunk and used the top bunk for a puzzle he was solving. The guards and I waited outside while he moved the puzzle to the desk and moved his mattress pad to the top bunk so I could use the bottom. Was this in deference to my old man appearance? I don't know, but I was thankful that I would be in a bunk instead of in a "boat." I entered the cell and the guards left the area. I introduced myself to my new cellmate, and I met Jason (not his real name).

Before the guards left, Jason asked if he could use the "boat" for a while. He said he was tired of sleeping on the hard bunk. The guard allowed him to get the "boat" and Jason placed it on the floor along the doorway of our cell. We would have to climb over the "boat" each time we exited the cell. The bunk beds were made of hardened steel and had no give to them in any way. Jason said he thought the "boat" would make a good change for him. He later found it was easier for him to watch television while lying in the "boat" versus lying in the bunk. It was all the same to me because it's not very enjoyable watching television through a steel mesh screen. However, I was appreciative I was not locked up in the neighboring cell. It did not have a view of the television or the outside at all.

Jason told me that we were allowed outside of our cells three times a day for an hour at a time. Usually these times were before lunch, in the afternoon and in the evening. Each cell was opened one at a time and those in that particular cell were the only ones allowed outside of their cells and into the "Dayroom."

Jason was a young man awaiting assignment to a boot camp for parole violation. We did not discuss the particulars of my case, but Jason understood from the guard that I had been moved to solitary because of death threats. Otherwise, throughout the day Jason read books and wrote letters, and our conversations remained of a general nature.

I anticipated our first break time. Jason told me it would occur about 10:00 A.M. The first cell was opened to our left and one inmate came out and sat in the "Dayroom" while his cellmate continued to lie in bed. In fact, I never saw the second inmate during my stay in solitary confinement. The first man talked to me and Jason a little and watched television. When his hour was up, he returned to his cell. When the cell door closed, Jason and I were allowed out of our cell.

Jason went straight to the one telephone mounted on the "Dayroom" wall and called his family. While he conversed with them, I paced the room back and forth, straightening my legs out and doing push-ups off of the walls, waiting for Jason to finish so I could call Alison. In about twenty minutes he finished and I immediately grabbed the phone and called Alison collect.

When she answered, the first thing I told her was that I had been transferred to solitary confinement. I didn't tell her about the death threats but she said she was so thankful that I had been moved. She expressed how worried she had been for me after the news broadcasts had been televised. She told me that she had talked with my sister and brother-in-law earlier that morning and they finally had the right papers together and were on their way to Conyers to give the bond for my release. She said she anticipated them arriving in Conyers about lunchtime. She told me about the difficulties they had been through with the authorities in both Oglethorpe and Rockdale County. She encouraged me greatly, especially when she said she felt confident that everything was finally going to work out and she hoped that I would be released that afternoon.

Despite being encouraged, having had my expectations up for release since Tuesday night caused me to only be cautiously hopeful. I knew from my attorney that if I did not obtain release by that afternoon, I would have to remain in jail until Monday, at least. Even though I felt greatly frustrated at the delays and the events that had occurred keeping me incarcerated, I was not in the least upset at any of my family nor Dr. Patterson because I knew they were doing all that they could to get me released.

After talking with Alison for a few minutes and our conversation was winding down, she said, "Before you go, someone wants to speak to you."

I had no idea who she might be talking about until a couple of moments later this sweet, soft, angelic, little girl's voice came over the line and said, "Hi, Pop."

It was my young granddaughter, Misty Jane. Before I could say, "Hi there, yourself," with a tremendous amount of difficulty, tears began to roll unashamedly down my cheeks. After a moment, I was finally able to ask her, "What are you doing in Georgia? You're supposed to be in Ohio!"

She gave a belly-shaking giggle and said, "I flew on an airplane with Grandma! I came here to stay with Grandma. When are you coming home, Pop?"

I tell you, I felt like openly weeping right there. I sniffled and said, "As soon as I can. You take care of Grandma until I get there, okay?"

She giggled again and said, "Okay. I love you, Pop."

Before I could tell her that I loved her too, she handed the telephone back to Alison. She made my heart leap in my chest when she said, "I was with Misty last night when she said her prayers and she said 'God, please get my Pop out of jail.' Can you believe she knew how to say that?"

You've got to believe that hearing those words made it very difficult to think about staying in jail any longer. Since being incarcerated Tuesday evening, I had not felt the emotional upheaval like I felt just then. A lot of poignant times had taken place, but none touched me like my little granddaughter.

Jason and I had not been back into our cell but for a few minutes when my name was called over the loudspeaker and I was informed that I had a visitor. This time, when I was escorted to the visitor's room, I was led through the jail library. I made a mental note to ask for permission to stop in there to look for a book when I returned to my cell.

Dr. Jerry Patterson was waiting for me. I sat down, picked up the telephone and looked at him through the glass. He picked up the telephone on his side of the glass and asked me how I was doing. I explained that I was now located in solitary confinement and felt much safer. Jokingly, I told him that he appeared awfully tired.

He laughed and said, "If we don't get you out of here soon, I don't know if my wife and I will ever get any sleep."

He started explaining how Carl and Beverly Martin, my brother-in-law and sister, had run into some difficulties getting my property bond accepted in Oglethorpe County. Apparently the size of the bond, $60,000, precluded anyone but the County Sheriff approving it. However, the Oglethorpe County Sheriff was not in town yesterday and was not available until that morning. Fortunately, Carl and Beverly had been able to meet the Sheriff earlier and he had signed off on the bond and they were now on their way to Conyers. Again, I remained cautiously hopeful remembering the other delays and roadblocks that had been incurred the previous three days.

We separated with him telling me he would be back in touch as soon as something definitively occurred. Returning to my cell, the guard walking with me allowed me to stop in the jail library, and I quickly picked up a couple of Western novels to read back in my cell. Shortly after returning, lunch was served and I spent the rest of the afternoon reading and talking with Jason. Jason expressed interest in some Scriptures he had been reading, and I was able to give a mini-Bible study. Also during quiet times, I prayed for continued strength and blessings on all of those trying to help me.

THE DOCTOR

Carl and Beverly Martin (Jim's brother-in-law and sister) became involved in the effort to obtain bond for Jim by using some property in the Athens, Georgia area. I had known this couple for almost as long as I had known Jim but had never been involved in any project with them until now. I found them to be a formidable pair. Beverly's gentle nature and acute insight along with Carl's refined tenacity coupled with his local connections finally prevailed, and bond was obtained.

I also had the opportunity of working with Garland Moore, Jim's attorney. I found he was always available when I called or he would return my calls in minimum time. He walked us through this whole ordeal, his assistance being invaluable.

THE SISTER

On Friday morning, Carl and I went back to the Sheriff's office around 9:30 A.M. The Sheriff was not there but was expected at some point. The same three people were in the office again as on the previous day and were as unhelpful as they were the day before. We went back outside of the Sheriff's office and waited for the Sheriff to drive up. We were hoping to catch him before he got inside with his staff. While we waited, Carl telephoned our attorney, Suzanne Burton, to see what other alternatives we would have, if any. She said she was prepared to meet us and with the Sheriff if need be to help us. She even called one of the men in the Sheriff's office and advised him the law stated that each county can recognize and accept a bond from one county to the other, dollar for dollar; but he, representing Oglethorpe County, still refused to acknowledge her admonishment.

The Sheriff finally arrived about 10:15 A.M. Carl is a former Marine and is accustomed to handling serious situations straight forward. As soon as we recognized the Sheriff's automobile, Carl walked rapidly toward him and met him as he climbed out of his car, telling the Sheriff what we needed. We went inside, he approved the bond and the papers were filled out and placed in a sealed envelope. We were told by one of his staff that the envelope was everything we would need for the bond. This was the same man who had been so uncooperative Thursday afternoon and Friday morning before the Sheriff arrived. It was 11:00 A.M.

We left the Sheriff's office and immediately began the approximate two hour trip to Conyers. Carl called Dr. Patterson to let him know we were on our way. He planned to meet us in Monroe, Georgia, approximately halfway from Conyers, to take the papers on to Conyers. After Dr. Patterson talked with Jim, he spoke to some of the Rockdale Jail personnel. The jail officers advised him that I would have to appear personally to authenticate the bond.

Thus, about forty-five minutes into our trip, Dr. Patterson called to say that someone at the Rockdale County Sheriff's Office said that I, personally, would need to bring in the papers because the property for bond was in my name. That didn't appear to present a problem. So at about 1:00 P.M., we met Dr. Patterson at the Rockdale County Jail to deliver the papers.

When the jail Captain opened the envelope, the only paper inside was the one signed by the Sheriff's office in Oglethorpe County. Another wall was thrown up at us!

An official with the Oglethorpe County Sheriff's Office was to have called Rockdale County to determine what was required to secure Jim's release. The notarized deed and payment of taxes statement had not been included. There appeared to be no other option but to return to Oglethorpe County, retrieve the proper documentation, and then return to Rockdale County, all before five o'clock. We were told that bonds would not be accepted after 5:00 P.M. Helpfully, we were told that anyone could present the papers for bonding out. So we quickly determined that Dr. Patterson would follow us to Oglethorpe County and then return with the appropriate papers.

I asked one of the jailers if I could see Jim to let him know what was going on. I was told it wasn't visitors' hours and that I would not be allowed to visit him. I then asked if I could write him a note and have it delivered to him. Again he denied my request. I said some pretty strong words and probably in a very loud voice for the jailer said, "He probably can hear you out here. He's sitting just behind us a few feet away in solitary confinement."

I don't know if Jim heard us or not, but I was frustrated that I couldn't let him know that we were doing all that we could do to get him released.

Unfortunately, we just kept running into these brick walls!

We had been driving back to Oglethorpe County for only about fifteen minutes when Carl received a call from the Rockdale County Captain. Carl had left our telephone numbers with him. The Captain advised Carl that we would need to provide one other document that stated there were no liens or judgments against the property being provided for bond. They couldn't understand that the house had been built and paid for without a loan ever being taken out against it. It was just one more thing that had to be done!

Carl first called the Oglethorpe County Clerk of Superior Court and explained the documentation that was needed. He was told that none of the personnel in the Clerk's office could provide that type of form. Carl then called our attorney, Suzanne Burton, but she had back to back property closings and could not help us. It was two o'clock now and our time was running out. We had to try and get to the Courthouse and back to Rockdale County jail before they closed. Dr. Patterson and Carl were continuously talking with each other, sharing the news of the latest development or holdup, speeding toward Oglethorpe County. Dr. Patterson had been in communication with Jim's attorney, Gary Moore, and confirming information from the Rockdale County Sheriff's Office. By now, I was feeling defeated because it looked as if we might not be able to get Jim out. I was sick to think he might have to stay in jail over the weekend.

We drove to our home and picked up copies of the deed and a tax statement, and then we drove to the

Sheriff's Office to meet Dr. Patterson. In the meantime, Dr. Patterson had called Jim's office to see if they could get someone to do the lien and judgment research at the courthouse. Jim had a researcher who lived in Oglethorpe County by the name of Amber Smith. They called Amber and she immediately drove to the Courthouse, and in less than thirty minutes she was able to provide a statement that my property was free and clear of any liens or judgments and therefore, was proper to be utilized for Jim's bond.

Carl picked up the document from Amber and found that our mother's pastor, Rev. Donald Wineinger, was there with her, expressing concern for Jim and asking if there was anything that he could do to help out. Then Carl met Dr. Patterson at the Sheriff's Office with all of the documentation together. While they were in the Sheriff's Office they contacted the Rockdale County jail and itemized the documents they had and were assured that they were appropriate. Finally, everything that Rockdale County required to secure bond was together with even a couple of extra forms just to be sure. Dr. Patterson took all of the documents and started the long drive back to the Rockdale County jail. I prayed he would make it in time.

THE ASSOCIATE

My defense of Jim seemed to grow from the moment this whole series of events started at the first of January right through his arrest. A case in point, I was in a county courthouse working in the deed room just a couple of days after his arrest. The overall opinion that I heard from others in the courthouse was one of disbelief. However, one gentleman's comments "flew all over me," as my mother would say. My "Holy Ghost" checked me and prevented me from embarrassing myself and this gentleman in front of several strangers and a few court clerks. He had said, "Supposedly he's innocent, but we don't know for sure." It wasn't what he said that upset me as much as the way he said it—with a smirk on his face and sarcasm in his voice.

So, being the diplomat that I am, I quietly asked him a question, but with a very direct tone in my voice.

"Hey, slick. How would you like for someone to give an anonymous tip to the local law enforcement people that you are involved in some 'not so reputable' dealings? Then let them come to your house and use a fine tooth comb to see what you've been up to?"

To my shock and amazement, he didn't particularly like my suggestion. Maybe because he has kids and doesn't know everything that has come across *his* computer screen. And the thought of serving five to twelve years for each count just didn't suit him very well. It didn't take long for most people who knew me to know where I stood on Jim's case.

THE CHAIRMAN

Sharing the same professional occupation, I was asked about Jim's status frequently. Many of our professional peers knew he and I attended the same church and was eager to hear of any new developments. Some asked with "knowing looks," others in total disbelief. My response to each question and inquiry was the same regardless of the number of times it was repeated, "If you knew Jim Reynolds the way I and many, many others know him and his character, you would be as certain as I am that there is no way he is guilty of these charges and allegations."

THE ACCUSED

Later, I learned that while I was spending a quiet afternoon in solitary confinement, my sister, brother-in-law and Pastor were being driven to fits trying to secure my bond. They had come to the Rockdale County jail prepared to present documents to secure my release but were informed by one the jail officers that they did not have all of the proper forms and statements; therefore, the property bond was not granted. All of that meant that they would have to drive approximately two hours back to Oglethorpe County, acquire the proper forms, and then drive the two hours back to Rockdale County.

My sister, Beverly, asked if she could see me, and the Deputy said, "No. It's not visiting hours."

Then Beverly asked if she could send me a note and the Deputy again said, "No."

Apparently a rather loud discussion then began to take place, as my sister and brother-in-law explained that all they wanted to do was tell me what was happening. The Deputy told them that I probably could hear them right then, as I was sitting just a few feet away in solitary confinement, directly behind where they were talking. It would have been very comforting if I could have heard them. Dismayingly, I did not hear anything.

As Carl and Beverly left the Rockdale County jail to proceed back to Oglethorpe County, Dr. Patterson decided to follow them back and then return with all of the proper paperwork, thus saving Carl and Beverly a return trip to Rockdale County. As they were traveling, the Rockdale County Sheriff's Office contacted Carl on his cell phone and advised him that one other piece of information would be required before my release. They needed a document declaring that the property in Oglethorpe County, being used for my property bond, was free and clear of any judgments or liens. It was now after 1:00 P.M. and they needed to have the documentation back to Rockdale County before 5:00 P.M., otherwise, I would have to remain incarcerated through the weekend. Carl, Beverly and Dr. Patterson almost became frantic. Dr. Patterson, however, called my office to see if they knew of someone who could issue such a document, and they certainly did.

Debbie Boyd, my office manager, contacted a title researcher who worked for Southern Courthouse Ventures Legal Research Firm, my company, by the name of Amber Smith. When Debbie told Amber what was needed, Amber said that she would meet Carl, Beverly and Dr. Patterson at the Oglethorpe County Courthouse and provide the documentation they needed.

The problem, which really wasn't a problem, was that the property that was to be used for my bond had never had a mortgage against it. My parents had purchased it and built a house on it without borrowing any money. They had lived there over twenty-five years. Amber performed the property search and then had a document notarized stating the property was free and clear of any liens or judgments. After securing that document and the other paperwork the Rockdale County Sheriff's Department required completing my property bond, Carl and Beverly gave it all to Dr. Patterson and he began his long trip back to Conyers. Fortunately, he didn't receive any speeding tickets, as far as I know!

Dr. Patterson arrived back at the Rockdale County jail just before 5:00 P.M. When he walked in, a shift change had occurred and he was met by a new duty officer. The officer asked Dr. Patterson why he was there, and Dr. Patterson explained that he had come to secure my release. Dr. Patterson then handed to the officer the envelope with all of the paperwork inside, wondering if he was going to run into another roadblock. The officer opened the envelope, glanced at the papers and asked, "What is all of this?"

Dr. Patterson explained that it was all of the paper-work requested to secure a property bond. The officer scanned through the documents and then looked up at Dr. Patterson and asked, "Is this all I need?"

Without hesitation Dr. Patterson simply answered, "Yes." After all that he had been through during the past four days attempting to secure my release, he wasn't about to give the Sheriff's Department any further reason to delay. He was told to wait in the jail lobby until I arrived.

As Dr. Patterson waited in the jail lobby, I was lying on my back reading. Without a warning, the loudspeaker crackled and a deep voice said, "Reynolds." I said, "Yes, sir," and the voice came back saying, "Pack up your things."

Well, I don't know if I set any speed records, but I think I had all of my necessities wrapped up in my sheets in about ten seconds. Though nothing was said about my being released, I was hopeful that was the reason I was being called. I just threw everything into the middle of the sheet, grabbed the corners ready to throw it over my shoulder and walk out. As I should have expected, the guards obviously weren't as prepared for me to leave as I was.

Jason said he was sad I was leaving and that he had been looking forward to my being a cellmate for a while. However, he said that he was glad I was getting out—it was the same thing he wanted. I told him that before I left I wanted to say a prayer for him if he would let me. He bowed his head and said, "Please do." I asked the Lord to keep His hands on Jason and protect him and help him to make good and wise choices in the future. That continues to be my prayer.

About ten minutes later, the outer cell door opened and then my cell door opened. A guard stood at the outer door, and he instructed me to follow him. As I walked out, I turned toward Jason and told him I would remember him in my prayers. I followed the guard back toward the section area.

For a moment I disappointingly thought I was going back to Section "C". I didn't know Dr. Patterson was waiting for me. I didn't know that my bond had been met. The voice over the loudspeaker had not said I was being released. I began wondering what in the world I was going to do if I was placed back into the general prison population.

We stopped short of the section doors at the storage area where I had picked up my sheets, blanket and necessities. The guard instructed me to place my linens in the laundry hamper. When I finished that, he told me to take my precious, priceless plastic cup back to the front desk. Again I was ordered to stand in the same spot where my world-famous photo had been taken. By this time, it was beginning to hit me that I was actually being released. Hallelujah!!

I continued standing there about five more minutes while the officers discussed my paperwork. Then, I watched as a guard placed clear plastic bags on the counter in front of me; bags holding the clothes I had worn to the jail the previous Tuesday night. The guard directed me to take my clothes to the restroom and change. I then turned in my cup, took the bags and went into the restroom. My quick change would have made the Superman of my youth proud. I was feeling an unnatural buzz—I was going home. I was getting out. *I'm being released. Praise God!!*

I could have made firemen proud in the speed I reached while changing clothes and dressing. Funny, all of my clothes were there except my belt. I stepped out of the restroom, set my orange coveralls and orange flip-flops on the counter. I signed several forms acknowledging that I was getting back everything that I brought into the jail. I was given a check for the cash I had brought in. Then a deputy, holding my belt in his hand, told me to follow him. He explained as we walked that it was a jail rule that a prisoner only receive his belt as he exits.

We reached the large sliding door that led into the lobby and waited for it to slide open. As it began to open, the deputy turned to me and handed me my belt, saying, "Here you go. Good luck." He turned, walked away, and I stepped through the doorway into the lobby where Dr. Patterson stood talking with a man. Dr. Patterson turned toward me, smiled and began ending his conversation with the other gentleman. I stood to the side and put on my belt. That's when I noticed my hands were shaking quite a bit. When the other gentleman walked off, Dr. Patterson turned to me and said, "I guess you're ready to go home."

I replied, "You just don't know how much."

It was approximately 5:45 P.M. when we stepped outside of the jail. The sun was setting, but the daylight was still clear and cool. I stopped at the first step and looked at the red-streaked sky, took a deep breath of the cold air and simply said with a shaky voice, "Thank you, Jesus." I could feel tears forming at the edge of my eyes and was thankful that Dr. Patterson and I were not trying to have a conversation as we walked toward his vehicle. I'm sure he saw and felt the emotions that were running through me, as the sensation that this part of my nightmare was truly over. I was free to go back home to my family.

As we got into his automobile, Dr. Patterson said that he needed to make a couple of phone calls. As he started to dial his cell phone, a wave of emotion went through me, and I remember grabbing his arm as I was shaking violently. Dr. Patterson patted my arm with his other hand and said, "I know, I know. It's okay. You're finally out and everything's going to be okay." Dr. Patterson telephoned Alison first, telling her that he would have me home in about twenty minutes.

He then called my sister, Beverly, who was at my mother's house. I overheard him telling her, "We finally got him out. He's sitting right here next to me."

I spoke a few words with her, my voice quivering. I arranged to meet them the next day and to see everyone. She began telling me she was so glad I was out and began apologizing profusely for the delay in obtaining my release. I told her that didn't matter to me; I was too grateful for all that everyone had done for me.

Dr. Patterson then called my attorney, Gary Moore, and told him I was released. I spoke with Gary for a few moments, and he informed me that in all of his years of practice, he had never seen so many road-blocks and difficulties that had developed in securing my release. He had told Dr. Patterson the same thing earlier. I later learned that throughout the time I was incarcerated, Gary had been in constant communication with my family and with Dr. Patterson. I was appreciative but yet humbled that so many people would do so many things to show that they cared for me and loved me. I did not think that I deserved such kindnesses and consideration.

Dr. Patterson pulled into my driveway, and who came out of my house running to greet me but my own precious little granddaughter, Misty Jane. I picked her up and hugged her hard and she hugged me back just as hard. AJ, Rob and Alison came out, hugged me, and commented, "You look good with a beard." I had forgotten that I had not shaved since the previous Tuesday morning. I'm sure I had a scraggily look.

Dr. Patterson left with the understanding we would meet in the morning, and he would go with me to see my mother and family in Oglethorpe County. He commented that he was looking forward to having a meal that my mother would prepare. Word apparently was getting around that I was released, for in just a few minutes, Debbie Boyd and her husband, JB, came to the house. Directly behind them came our good friends, Bo and Gail Chandler. They even brought some great food with them, but I was unable to enjoy very much of it; I guess I was still on my jailhouse diet! Everyone was expressing their happiness that I was home but were also wondering where all of this was leading.

Shortly afterwards, I walked next door to the home of our neighbors of seven years, Ed and Linda Baker. During the news media frenzy, Linda Baker had been interviewed and was shown on television as a staunch defender of me. I had been told that she mounted a great defense of my name. I went over and expressed my gratitude for what she had done.

Later, several of my friends sent her cards of thanks, and Alison and I sent her flowers.

While I was visiting the Bakers, Gary Moore came in. He had come home, crossed the street to see me and had learned I was next door. He shared with us his discontent with the media and the difficulties of securing a property bond. Shortly thereafter, Gary and I walked out together and stood in the street between our houses discussing the future just as we had done on previous but less stressful occasions. Gary told me to be patient as it might be several weeks before we knew what we were facing. He expressed confidence that we could mount more than an adequate defense when the time came.

I went back inside my house. Alison wanted to prepare me a meal, but I declined. I told her I just wanted to lie down in a real bed. I talked with AJ and Rob, who had interrupted their ski trip to be with their mother when they learned I had been incarcerated. I got to talk with Misty Jane before she ran off to bed. After soaking in a hot tub until the water turned cold, I lay down thanking God for keeping me and then slept a solid ten hours.

THE DOCTOR

The day I met Jim when he was finally released from jail, was uneventful except for the tremendous sense of relief that both of us felt when we finally walked out of the Rockdale County Jail facility. Jim was so relieved when we sat down in my car that he was visibly shaking. We actually had prayer, and his frustrations diminished and a calmness and a peace came over him almost instantly. We drove to his home where his family met and embraced him. I was relieved that this part of the nightmare was over. I drove home feeling the same sense of relief and peace that Jim felt.

THE SISTER

A little before 6:00 P.M. we got a phone call from Dr. Patterson telling us that Jim was out. I simply thanked God.

CHAPTER 12

THURSDAY, JUNE 29, 2006
THE ACCUSED

I began the next two and a half year journey by rising early on Saturday morning, January 31, 2004. I rode with my pastor, Dr. Jerry Patterson, to my mother's home, about an hour and a half from my home. Having been a minister and a friend to my family for decades, I knew that Dr. Patterson's presence would be a comfort to those of my family who would be at my mother's home as we discussed what had happened and the uncertain future. As we drove down the road, he and I discussed how I should talk to my family, and we decided that I should tell them starting at the point where pop-ups and spam began appearing on my computers. He felt that by sharing this information my family would feel better about the whole situation and would be more supportive with what lie ahead.

We reached my mother's home early and enjoyed a scrumptious lunch with her, my sister and brother-in-law, and my mother's pastor, Rev. Donald Wineinger. After lunch, other members of my family joined us: my nephew, Chuck Martin, and his wife Wendy; my nephew, Scott Martin, and his wife, Sue, and my niece, Sherri Poole. We gathered in my mother's living room where I sat on the couch with Dr. Patterson on one side of me and Reverend Wineinger on the other side. All the others sat around me as I began my dissertation.

It was very emotional for me from the very beginning. Here sat most of my family, the closest human beings to me, and I felt that I had failed them and embarrassed them beyond measure. I first apologized that I was causing them so much trouble and distress and I hoped that they would understand what had happened. I explained to them that I believed that the trouble all began in late 2002 when, after undergoing open heart surgery earlier that year and suffering certain difficult aftereffects, I investigated the potential of Viagra and whether or not I was a candidate for its use. I had decided that before approaching my family physician, I would research the drug on the Internet. I did not remember the exact date when I performed the research, but I did remember that this was the first time I had seen pornography on my computer.

I described to them how I researched the name "Viagra" and information concerning the drug and its possible effects to someone in my condition. When I finished reading the material and had made my notations for discussion with my doctor, I clicked the spot to close the page. Suddenly, a pop-up appeared. It was an advertisement for other similar drugs but was much more provocative in its depiction in that it displayed semi-clad couples. I glanced at the ad and then simply clicked to close it. That's when another pop-up appeared. Having experienced other pop-ups advertising insurance, mortgages, banks and fantastic trips to Las Vegas, this was becoming just plain aggravation to me. I was not interested in any further information or interested in reading any other advertisements. I was finally able to close the screen out and walked away thinking nothing further of the pop-ups.

I explained that before this time, the pop-ups had involved advertisements announcing various mort- gage companies and their rates, insurance companies, banking services and occasional travel enticements. But over the course of the next year, the sex-oriented pop-ups increasingly grew in number and explicit- ness. Both my family and office staff reported seeing advertisement pop-ups and the various attempts to establish firewalls and pop-up blockers seem to work only temporarily. As the pop-ups and spam continued, they gradually grew from just mild, semi-clad type depictions to the most vile and gross pictures imag- inable. I could remember seeing one pop-up ad that showed an image that made my stomach physically churn, it was so upsetting.

I told them further of the different computer tech- nicians I had hired to install firewall protection and blockers. As I mentioned earlier, these would appear to work for a while and then the pop-ups would begin again. At times, several pop-ups would appear at the same time, so many that at times they would appear as a cascade of playing cards across the screen. I told them of how one of the computer technicians described a virus that was in one of our computers that whenever the computers were turned off, the virus was programmed to regenerate itself and start all over again when the computer was turned back on. Another technician tracked a computer virus back to an e-mail we had received from one of our clients to my company. Apparently that client had contracted the virus and had unknowingly passed it on to us and it had infected our computers. When someone in my office had opened that particular e-mail, the virus had been attached and downloaded to one of our computers which then spread to other computers.

I expressed to my family the frustration that came from constantly battling this and that at times it seemed the situation was just going to be one that we would have to put up with and adjust to. I repeated what one technician had told me that since our computers were operating on DSL and was on 24-7, it made them more vulnerable to viruses and spam and other computer attacks. If I could learn of another way to operate my business efficiently without enduring this constant bombardment of pop-ups, I was more than willing to find out how.

I admitted to them that I had looked at some of the pictures when they popped-up over the months, shocked at what I saw. It was simply out of morbid curiosity that I looked, but that I had never purchased, traded or ordered any pornography of any description. I confessed that I was as human as any man and when confronted with pictures of naked women I had looked at them but not out of a sense of desire.

I concluded my discussion with my family and friends with the discovery of the credit card numbers that were used to create a child pornography website. I also explained that whoever had hacked into my computer had gotten that credit card number through my use of that credit card over the internet to purchase books and historical documents. I explained that my attorney had evidence and was gathering even more to show that my computer had been hacked into and my identity used to create the website. I assured them that I was not guilty of purchasing pornography of any kind much less owning and operating a pornography website. I ended by telling them that my attorney had said that while it only takes very little evidence to cause an arrest that it takes an extreme larger amount to call for an indictment much less a conviction.

Everyone there expressed their love, support and their confidence in me. They said they were sorry that this was happening to me, regardless, they were willing and able to defend me and help in any way that they could. I guess only eternity can reveal how much their love, concern and words encouraged me, and I know that I'll never be able to express my appreciation enough.

As folks were leaving, I stood on the front porch of my mother's house and talked with her Pastor. Rev. Donald Wineinger had been my mother's minister for a number of years and she was constantly bragging on his preaching and expressed a lot of confidence in him. I told him that I was concerned about how all of my troubles were going to affect my mother and her health, emotionally and physically. He assured me that he would stay in contact with her and would talk with her from time to time and reassure her. He said he didn't believe in the accusations against me and would do anything that he could to help me out. He provided constant comfort to my mother during my ordeal and continues to maintain my mother's bragging rights.

THE FRIEND

By the time Jimmy's bond was set and he was released, he was an emotional wreck. When we talked, he would weep and I could see that the light that had always been in his eyes before was gone. He now held his head down and his shoulders slumped. This was a broken man, and it made me mad.

How could this have happened? I said to him on many occasions that this was crazy, none of it made any sense. They had to have the wrong person; there must be another Jimmy Reynolds involved somewhere else or a virus in his computer. Jimmy's attorney had said it was identity theft, and Jimmy believed someone must have gotten his identification and opened a website. I was still so angry just to watch such a good man try to make sense of all of this.

It was just not fair.

THE SISTER

During the weeks and months following Jim's arrest, my main concern was for his mental and emotional health. I was also concerned for his physical wellbeing, concerned for what the stress and strain would put on his heart after his having several heart attacks and bypass surgery. My only recourse was prayer because I knew there was nothing Carl and I could do for him otherwise, except give him love and support and that all the answers were in God's hands.

For the first year, my prayer was that the charges would be dismissed completely. As time dragged on, I realized my prayer was too specific, so I started praying, "Thy will be done and help us to accept your will."

Each time we saw Jim or I talked with him on the telephone, he tried to make us feel better, trying to be optimistic. I could see in his eyes and hear in his voice what a toll this ordeal was having on him. During the proceeding weeks and months, I agonized over the possibility of a Grand Jury appearance for Jim and thought about all of the ramifications that this would have on Jim and the whole family. Jim's attorney kept assuring Jim and Jim passed on the news to us that the longer it took for the case to go before the Grand Jury, the better it looked that there would be no case. This was hard to believe, but I kept praying in faith for all of us and for God's will.

THE ACCUSED

Up to that point, I had not made an appearance in the general public, only to my close family and my neighbors. I had not been out in society to gauge their reaction and to discover what my feelings would be like. But that was not to be for very much longer. For almost as soon as I returned home from my mother's and Dr. Patterson dropped me off, my wife, Alison, received a telephone call from her brother, Jamie, telling her that their mother, Jane Broome, had suffered a stroke earlier that afternoon and was hospitalized.

We immediately prepared to travel to St. Joseph's Hospital in Atlanta where Jane had been admitted. Alison and I, along with AJ, Rob and Misty boarded our Ford Explorer and, as we drove off, discovered we needed fuel. We stopped at a self-service filling station and as Rob filled our tank, I said I would go inside the convenience store and pay for the gas. As I began walking toward the pay station, I suddenly felt very vulnerable and overexposed. I sensed that everyone was looking at me. My picture had just appeared on the front page of the local newspaper, *The Rockdale Citizen*, only two days prior. Were people recognizing me? Was someone going to point toward me and whisper to someone else standing next to them? Was someone going to walk up to me and ask, "Say, didn't I see your picture in the paper?" Those questions and more were running through my head in a myriad of fear.

Dressed for the cold, I walked into the service station with my head down, tucked deep into my overcoat. I stood behind a couple of other people for a few moments, paid for the gas without saying a word and quickly turned and walked out. I walked rapidly to my SUV and quickly got in, thankful to be back with my family and hidden by the vehicle walls and tinted glass.

As I was driven to the hospital I began to wonder in my mind, *Is this how it's going to be from now on? Am I going to constantly dread going out in public? Will I always be afraid to see people or meet people from now on? Will I be suspicious of people? Will they be suspicious of me? Will people be wondering about me and be ugly to me before they find out their suspicions are untrue and find out the truth of what's going on?*

I almost decided to simply sit in the Explorer while everyone else went into the hospital, but Jane had been wonderful to me and had been a great mother-in-law, always treating me with love and respect. It was an honor to be her son-in-law and I owed her all of the support that I could give to her. It was more important for me to let her know that I cared and was concerned for her than what I thought other people were thinking about me. While I felt severe misgivings being in a public place and seeing other people, particularly strangers, my brother-in-law, Jamie, appears to have been the only other one there who knew of my arrest. The only mention made of my arrest was when Jamie asked if I was doing okay and that he didn't believe any of the charges and that he would do anything that he could to help me out.

Thankfully, through God's blessings, Jane Broome was soon dismissed from the hospital and, after a great deal of physical therapy over several months, eventually recovered and continues to live a very active life.

For the next several weeks, it was a constant, daily battle within my own mind just to force myself to maintain any type of regular routine, especially when it involved stepping out beyond the bounds of my own home. I was afraid to go out into public. I feared meeting strangers who might recognize me from the news stories on television and in the newspapers. I dreaded even the idea of seeing people who only vaguely knew me and observing the looks that might appear on their faces. I was frustrated at what people would think about me when they saw me and their odious suspicions. I really had no way to defend myself from the thoughts people would have concerning the accusations levied against me and the resulting publicity of my arrest. My emotions were ravaged by the thought that upon hearing that I had been arrested, many people would go ahead and judge me guilty without the benefit of hearing all of the facts. While my family and several of my friends had been adamant in expressing their support and confidence in me, I was wary when it came to acquaintances and those who scarcely knew me. What were they thinking? What were their reactions going to be upon seeing me? What were they going to say to their family and friends about me? How were my employees going to handle the coming days? Were there going to be any repercussions from any of my clients? Could my business and my family survive the onslaught surrounding this incident?

While the answers to those questions and even more that I had not even thought of yet would only come with time, one answer came the very next day, Sunday, February 1, 2004. I decided to go ahead and attend services at Faith Tabernacle located in Conyers, Georgia. My wife, Alison, was not able to attend because she had to prepare our granddaughter, Misty, for her return trip to Ohio. So, I drove to the church alone. I didn't know what to expect when I entered the church lobby, but immediately I was surrounded by members of the church and friends telling me they were so glad I had been released and that I had decided to come on to church. They all asked as to my welfare and assured me that they would continue to hold me up in prayer. I was shunned by no one, that I could tell, but even more so I was embraced by several of the men and women and was told that I was loved. Throughout the church service, the feeling of being stared at was overwhelmed by the love and care I had felt from the members of the congregation, so much so that I wished I could have just stayed in church until my whole ordeal was over. It was through those people that God showed His love and through them He spoke to me words of comfort and safety.

The next day I worked at my office the whole day, trying to put some of my worries and concerns out of mind through business activities. Early the next morning, Dr. Patterson called me and asked me to have lunch with him at a local steakhouse. With great trepidation, I accepted his offer and met him at noon. As he and I walked through the restaurant, I could not help but notice a man sitting at a nearby table staring at me intently. His eyes followed me as I sat down. The man never said a word to me, just stared. He was so bold that when I looked at him he did not cut his eyes away from me but continued to gaze at me. It is possible he recognized me and maybe he was trying to figure out from where. I made a comment to Dr. Patterson about the man and he said that my story had not been repeated in the news and that other events were making headlines now. He continued by saying that except for the people who knew me, the news concerning my arrest was going to quickly fade from the minds of everyone else. As I thought about the logic of his statements, I felt some better. It would later occur to me that by inviting me to lunch, Dr. Patterson was helping me to ease back into the public arena.

Over the coming days, I would go back into the area courthouses to continue my business functions. I was mostly in the company of Sean Peacock, continuing his training that had been interrupted by my arrest. Being with him helped me to feel protected and immune to the shunning I endured from some folk. Early on, some people that I saw in the courthouses ignored me or would not acknowledge my presence nor return my greetings. They were individuals who did not know me well, and eventually I accepted the fact that they did not have a full understanding of my situation and were reacting with cautiousness, not wanting to appear overly friendly to a man that potentially faced a very high publicity trial, if not conviction.

Throughout the whole two and half year ordeal, there were those in both my church and in the court-houses who never one time asked about my case nor approached me with inquisitiveness. It was not that they didn't care but I later heard from several of them that from the very beginning, they had assumed that because I continued to work in the courthouses, attend church services and that I was not locked up, that they simply accepted that either the case was over or that I would tell them differently. Then there were those individuals that I would run into occasionally who never failed to ask about the status of my case, not out of a desire to gossip but out of a sincere concern. They would many times respond to my declarations that nothing was happening with a "There's nothing to it," or "I felt like there was a mistake all along." Mostly I found that these people continued to interact with me on a normal basis regardless of the publicity and the sometime negative remarks from those who did not know me well.

THE FRIEND

From the time of Jimmy's arrest and release and throughout the coming months and years, some of the men from our church would approach me from time to time and ask me how I felt about Jimmy's situation and what I thought was going to happen. I always gave them the same answer, "There is no way that any of this can be true. He'll be exonerated someday."

As they watched him over time, he pulled himself up over his many trying obstacles, and they recognized that this man was truly innocent.

THE DOCTOR

I met with Jim and Alison many times over the next few months, and we considered all of the consequences of what was happening in their lives. We discussed the personal, moral, spiritual and relational dynamics, as well as the legal situation as the information became available for us through Jim's attorney, Gary Moore.

For obvious reasons, I will not reveal much of what transpired in our sessions as they were deeply personal and extremely sensitive, however, I will share some of my observations about their remarkable strength as they went through this very difficult time in their lives.

Alison resisted the natural tendency to 'blame' in this situation and honestly sought to understand how it could have happened and how to best use her energies to get through this ordeal. I sincerely appreciated her desire to understand, as opposed to her wanting to engage in the futile effort of blame, as it made my job in counseling much less difficult.

Alison continued to be understanding and non-judgmental in her willingness to work through this with Jim. However, I did get the feeling that should such charges ever be found to be true, her position would have been equally strong in insisting that the matter be dealt with appropriately. She only once expressed as much, but she did this in a manner that left no doubt in my mind as to her meaning.

Throughout the weeks and months following Jim's arrest, I never found that Alison changed from the first time I talked with her. She handled the stress of the long, drawn out, two plus years matter with the same grace and dignity that I came to expect from her. She has the ability to be candid, honest and, on occasion, even direct, but always caring and supportive. Jim has a great deal to appreciate in the lady he has chosen to be his wife.

THE ACCUSED

Everyday, in some shape, manner or form, I would be reminded, if in nothing else but within my own mind, that I was unjustly accused of the most gross and most insidious crimes. I would be reminded that there were going to be some people who were going to believe the accusations without ever giving me the benefit of a doubt. I was also reminded that I didn't have the slightest clue how this whole thing was going to turn out.

And then every night there were the dreams.

In orange.

Always orange.

Many times I would awaken during the night from dreaming of being in a cell again, always wearing orange. I would dream of being in other places, in the public, wearing orange.

Orange.

Always orange.

There were times that if I saw someone wearing orange, I would actually cringe, reminded of my ordeal in jail. I did not look for orange, but it seemed that no matter where I went I would somehow run into someone wearing orange. From clothes to highway signs, from advertisements to candy, I always seemed to be running into something orange. I sometimes felt like the color was following me around and that I was going to be incapable of escaping it.

Orange.

Always orange.

THE FRIEND

I watched as Jimmy rode an emotional roller coaster that kept him going up and down. I never knew how I would find him the next time I would see him and we would talk with each other. More times than not, he only needed someone to listen to him.

THE ACCUSED

A singular occurrence will serve to demonstrate how paranoid I had become and how just a simple, normal event could effect my emotions. Fortunately, it didn't involve the color orange. One evening, a few weeks after my arrest, I decided to take my wife, Alison, out to dinner. As we pulled from our subdivision onto a county road, I noticed a Rockdale County Sheriff's car pulling in behind us. I turned to the left and he followed. I reached the access road parallel with I-20, turned onto it, and the Sheriff's car was still behind me. I pulled into the restaurant parking lot and the Sheriff's car drove on by. Coincidence? Mistake? Luck? Maybe, but I felt uncomfortable, nevertheless.

We left the restaurant to return home, and then my paranoia kicked into overdrive. It became paranoia unplugged. As I crossed under a traffic signal, the reflection of street lights revealed another Sheriff's car behind us. Oh no, not again! I mentioned this to Alison but she did not remark about it until at another traffic signal, I turned right. She asked if the car was still behind me and I acknowledged that it was. The automobile remained behind us until we arrived at the entrance to our subdivision and he passed behind us.

Throughout the two and a half year misery, regular appearances of Sheriff patrol cars in my neighborhood would cause me to be momentarily dismayed and nervous. I felt like I was acting guilty when I was only trying to maintain a normal existence. But the trauma of being arrested and the notoriety gained from the news media continued to torment me, and emotionally I was becoming drained. Only God's grace kept me from suffering a nervous breakdown.

While I waited for the legal system to do whatever it was going to do with the accusations levied against me, I tried my best to continue on with my life in all areas as normally as possible. My company continued to prosper but not at the same pace as it had enjoyed prior to my arrest. Though I could not point to any specific client ceasing to do business with Southern Courthouse Ventures Legal Research Firm due to my arrest, the next two and a half years found my company maintaining the same level of income as the year 2003. We lost some clients but we also replaced them with new ones. I can only look back and realize that any lack of business growth during that time was owing to my own emotional state of mind and my inability to remain enthusiastic for any length of time due to the uncertainty of my circumstances. I thank God for my staff members and associate researchers who showed great loyalty and support. When some of my office staff left for positions with other companies, these were normal and expected transitions. New staff members, like Amy Pilcher and Jerry Eskew, came on board knowing the circumstances surrounding me but have proved their trustworthiness and friendship on numerous occasions.

The only really negative occurrence business-wise happened in March 2006. I went to the Rockdale County Courthouse to the Clerk of Superior Court Office to make application to renew my Notary Public certificate, an office I have held for over thirty years. When I turned in my renewal application, I was advised by one of the Deputy Clerks that my application would be reviewed by the Clerk of Superior Court and that I would be notified by mail. Two days later I received a letter from the Clerk of Superior Court informing me that they were, "...holding this application until the pending charges against you in Rockdale Superior Court are disposed of, at which time I will consider the renewal." I relayed this information to my attorney, who in turn contacted the Clerk of Superior Court, advising them that after two plus years since my arrest, no indictment had been brought, no pleadings had been given, and that otherwise, I was fully qualified to serve as a Notary Public, based upon the requirements of the State of Georgia. The Clerk of Superior Court stated that they reserved the right to withhold approval of any renewal request that they deemed under question. While he disagreed with that right they claimed, my attorney advised me to simply wait. As it was to occur, my application was quickly approved within days of dismissal of all charges.

THE CHAIRMAN

Jim suffered the loss of some acquaintances and some business relationships. And while he has always been a man of faith, his faith was tried almost to the breaking point. Not only had he suffered because of the evil and vile actions of someone else, his family suffered greatly also.

THE DOCTOR

Jim's attitude was never one of hostility, neither toward the law enforcement officials or the media, nor toward the jailers after his confinement. He focused on how to get through this, put an end to it, and move on with his life. It was to this end that we devoted the larger part of our time together. Through the many hours we spent together, Jim never faltered in his effort to work through this nightmare, and he never suggested giving up or settling with the District Attorney's Office. I was amazed at his patience.

THE ACCUSED

In spiritual matters, I remained faithful in my attendance to Faith Tabernacle and after a time became a member and secretary of the church funding committee, Wise Men Give Him Gifts. The other seven members of the Committee—Jay Barwick, Rev. Clell Eskew, Steve Hardy, Dr. James Harper, Dennis Hudson, Ricky Patterson and Steve Rosser— accepted me in their group, and we shared many joyful times together working on various projects.

Wherein in the past I occasionally visited other churches, I felt constrained and uncomfortable with the thought of going to any other churches due to the depression and paranoia I endured because of my case. Several pastors and ministers that had known me for a number of years extended me an open invitation to visit them and their churches; regrettably, I did not accept any of their offers. I still felt very self-conscious and somewhat intimidated and paranoid of meeting people and trying to explain my arrest. I have to admit that there were times that I became weary of offering explanations and appearing to defend or justify myself.

One effect that preyed on my mental thinking and on my social behavior at the same time was that I found myself uncomfortable in the presence of children. I found myself consciously not speaking or even looking at a child. I found it uncomfortable to even comment on the birth of a new baby for fear my comments would be misunderstood. I feared that my intentions would be questioned if I complimented a child or spoke favorably about a child's accomplishments. Never one time did anyone, particularly in my church, ever appear uncomfortable in my presence when children were around—I was the one who seemed to feel all of the constraint and pressure. This was just an example of the unsavory consequences undergone by the position I found myself in.

Although I was very blessed in that I did not suffer any overt rejection, except in the isolated cases involving a few individuals that I worked alongside in the area courthouses, there was one source of rejection that caused me a lot of anguish. This came from a particular minister with whom I felt I had a close and personal relationship, a relationship that had been established through other heartaches and troubles. It proved to be very distressful to me when, soon after I was arrested, I was not contacted by this minister, and throughout the remainder of the time this awful situation lasted, he did not call, write, or communicate with me at all. When family members, friends and even casual acquaintances would take the time to offer words of encouragement and support, the silence from this minister was deafening and disheartening. I waited and watched for a year in hopes he would contact me, but afterwards I decided that he must have been too embarrassed and ashamed of me to talk with me. Or was it possible that he believed I was guilty of the charges and accusations and he wanted nothing to do with me?

Soon after the dismissal was issued, I contacted this minister and we met privately where I told him of my distress. He sincerely and profusely apologized, explaining his lack of contact was simply not knowing what to say to me. He told me that on a number of occasions, he thought about calling but just didn't follow through, not understanding all that I was going through and was afraid he could not offer any further help. Our discussion helped me to realize that among those who appeared to be reluctant to converse with me were probably many who felt the same way. The whole situation was unrealistic and they were probably incapable of discerning a proper response. They weren't being mean or intentionally cold or aloof, they simply just didn't know how to react or what to say. Thankfully, God kept my heart tender and willing to give as much forgiveness to others as I have received from Him. God helps all of us to resist holding grudges and letting peace and love reign in our hearts.

THE CHAIRMAN

The months would come and go and Jim's case would not be brought before a Grand Jury. Jim's desire to fight to clear his name showed intensely in his eyes and in the tone of his voice every time we talked about it. This waiting, not knowing when "the shoe was going to fall" wore heavily upon him. It was really more than he alone could bear and withstand.

I was so humbled that there were occasions when he felt comfortable enough to talk with me about his situation, especially during those times when he felt he could no longer move forward. He would ask, "Why won't they move and give me a chance to defend myself?"

We would talk; I would pray for him often. He was upheld in prayer by many, many others and eventually God brought him through this horrible ordeal.

THE ACCUSED

In the past I had been active socially and politically in my community. With the accusations and the sensational press coverage of my arrest, I withdrew from active participation with many social groups— again, not because anyone rejected me or told me not to be involved but because of my own feelings of humiliation and embarrassment, and certainly, paranoia. While I was taught as a child not to ever worry about what other people thought, it was impossible not to be concerned with what was being contemplated about me. And by proxy, what was being thought of my family and friends. Despite the best efforts of my family and friends to defend and protect me, there was one overt incident that affected me strongly.

I had been a member of a particular historical and genealogical organization for over twenty years. I had served as an officer in this organization, elected to and appointed to local, state and national levels. At one time, I had served as the top officer in Georgia. Through this organization, I had developed many relationships both in Georgia and many other states, and throughout my legal ordeal several of them proved faithful and true friends. However, on February 6, 2004, I was to be greatly heart stricken. I received a certified letter with this organization's name on the outside. As I opened the envelope, I was thinking to myself that I must be receiving a note of support and encouragement from the local club. For, many times in the past, I had worked on numerous projects and donated both time and money to the local group in helping others. I thought this was to be their way of returning thanks, but I was sorely disappointed.

The letter stated, "The Executive Committee… respectfully request your resignation…" It went on further to read, "This action is being done to preserve the good name of… (the group)." To say the least, I was stunned in as much this was totally unexpected. I was heartbroken and hurt tremendously for I felt that my expenditures of time, talent, energy and finances for this organization should have been more respected and appreciated. Instead, they turn their backs on me in a time when I could have used their friendship and encouragement. This was totally disabusing and debilitating.

I responded to their letter on February 12, 2004, with a registered letter of resignation from all levels of the organization and attached a personal missive in part stating, "You have obviously 'rushed to judgment' and determined I was guilty and deserved no less than expulsion." I concluded with a request that at a future time that I be afforded an opportunity to address the organization with the whole story. I also recommended that should another incident occur similar to mine that they should, "…consider waiting until all of the evidence to be known before rushing a decision such as you have made concerning me."

With my family, I went through cycles of almost total withdrawal to eventually being able to travel with some comfort of mind. On Monday evening following my release from jail the previous Friday, I visited my daughter's jewelry store in Conyers, called the "Joy of Jewelry." My daughters, Joy and Jenna, were there along with their mother, Jennifer. While they were aggravated that they had to find out through the newspapers that I had been arrested, they accepted my explanation that when I was informed I was to turn myself in that I thought it would only be for a short time. I had wanted to explain the situation to them myself, in person. I told them I was sorry that they had to find out the way that they did, but that was not how I had planned it. I certainly did not want them to find out about my arrest through the newspapers or from anywhere else for that matter. They understood the series of events and articulated their shock and concern for everything that had happened. Throughout the remainder of my ordeal, they consistently expressed their love and support, and they were a constant source of strength and encouragement.

To demonstrate how devastating my arrest and subsequent media attention had affected my ability to function normally and respond to events with capability, just a week after my release, on Saturday, February 7, 2004, my former mother-in-law, Christine

Colquitt, passed away after a long illness. She had always been a good and kind woman to me and had always treated me with respect. Certainly, I truly wanted to pay my respects to her and especially for the sake of my daughters, Joy and Jenna, and their mother, Jennifer. With the thoughts of attending visitation or her funeral services, knowing that a number of family and friends would be there and that I would probably prove to be more of a distraction rather than a source of comfort, I was totally incapable of having the courage and fortitude to attend. I became nervous just thinking about trying to handle all of the possible questions many of them would ask. I endured severe disappointment that I could not show Christine's family and friends that I respected her and I wish that I could have express my sympathies in person. I trust that my card of condolences sufficiently expressed my sorrow and regrets at the passing of Christine.

One aspect of this terrible ordeal I was enduring that I was finally able to face was to see the local newspaper article concerning my arrest. I downloaded the information from the internet at the *Rockdale County Citizen* website. They had placed a color picture of my arrest photo on the front page at the very top beside the headline that read, "Conyers Businessman Faces Child Porn Charges." The article stated that the Rockdale County Sheriff's Office investigators had arrested me for allegedly having "numerous images" containing child pornography on five computers used in my home and business. It further stated I faced 12 felony charges of sexual exploitation of children after the GBI had contacted the Sheriff's office after they in turn had been contacted by officials of the National Center for Missing and Exploited Children concerning a possible website out of Rockdale County. The article also quoted the Rockdale County Sheriff as saying, "The Internet allows anonymity for this type of behavior. It could be someone in your neighborhood who seems like the most normal person in the world. However, there is technology out there for law enforcement to counteract it, and we will use it." The article concluded that I was being held in the Rockdale County Jail on $60,000 bond.

I could only imagine the embarrassment my family members must have felt when they saw this. I could only imagine what my friends were thinking. I could not imagine that I could suffer any more humiliation than what I felt right then. I was so ashamed that I could be accused of such a heinous and awful crime. But I knew I had to endure to the best of my ability and not allow my integrity to become abused any more than it had. I resolved to do all that I could to restore my name and absolve my family from the embarrassment I had caused them.

Fortunately, my emotional state settled to a more normal pace, and I was able to participate and enjoy a grand family occasion. On March 26, 2006, my sister, Beverly, and her husband, Carl Martin, celebrated their Fiftieth Wedding Anniversary. They held a vow renewal ceremony at a small church in Oglethorpe County, pastored by a good friend of mine, Rev. Chuck Tatum. The family had asked me to conduct the vow renewals, and though I suffered a certain amount of apprehension, it was a great honor to share this moment with them and many friends and family members. By the time the ceremony and reception had finished, I could tell that a certain amount of confidence had returned and replaced the earlier trepidation.

Dr. Patterson and I restarted our usual Thursday morning meetings over breakfast. Our conversations would dwell on the status of the investigation and my own emotional state of mind. His continued support, faithfulness and friendship greatly contributed to maintaining my equilibrium, balance and mental sanity. While God deserves all of the Glory for keeping me, I know that the Lord used Dr. Patterson to encourage me, comfort me and lift me up.

As for the case itself, throughout the coming long months, my attorney, Gary Moore, kept me informed of any developments and advised me of any information he was able to obtain. Early on he stated that we would not be able to look at any of the evidence being developed by the District Attorney's Office until after the case was presented to the Rockdale County Grand Jury. If that presentation was ever made, neither he nor I would be there during the hearing; we would not be able to offer any defense or explanation. The situation would be one wherein the District Attorney would present his evidence in order to convince the Grand Jury to call for a trial. Afterwards, if the Grand Jury rendered a "true bill" and ordered a trial, my attorney could then review the evidence and develop a proper rebuttal and defense. Until that time, not knowing all that the District Attorney may have developed as evidence, Gary worked on various defense approaches anticipating the thrust of the District Attorney's case.

I communicated with Gary Moore any information that came to me. For instance, I advised him that my office manager, Debbie Boyd, had been interviewed by the GBI and the Rockdale County Sheriff's Department on Thursday, February 12, 2004, and my wife, Alison, the next day. I think others were also interviewed.

On Thursday, February 19, 2004, I received a telephone call from Alison's son, AJ, who was living in Dayton, Ohio, that proved to be very encouraging and caused me to be very hopeful that maybe this nightmare would end soon. Earlier, investigators with the Georgia Bureau of Investigation had talked with him concerning my visits to Ohio and my visits with him and his family. They questioned him as to whether or not I had used their computers and Internet access. They asked if I had ever used their telephone to call anyone, particularly in Ohio. They wanted to know if I had ever gone off by myself or been left alone or if they had discovered me talking to anyone they didn't know or recognize. They inquired about a visit to the Cincinnati Zoo we had made the previous year and whether I had made any other visits to Cincinnati. Of course, every response from AJ was in the negative. He was able to tell them that I had never used their computers, their telephones and had not received any unusual calls or visits from anyone.

Then their questions changed as they began to ask about any knowledge he might have concerning a particular name. The investigators indicated to AJ that this person was one of particular interest to them and that this person's name had come up while they were investigating my computers. They also indicated that apparently this particular individual was being further investigated by other agencies in regard to some illegal websites. It appeared they were trying to establish a relationship, whether personal, professional or financial, between myself and an individual that lived in Cincinnati, Ohio, who was suspected of owning and operating illegal websites, probably child pornography related. When AJ asked if I had ever heard of the name before, I answered that the name meant absolutely nothing to me—I did not recognize the name at all.

Advising my attorney, Gary Moore, of this development, he said this would probably mean that their investigation would continue through the summer and possibly into September 2004. He said that they would probably not reveal this information in their presentation to the Grand Jury, but it would certainly warrant attention from him in our defense. He said he would continue developing other options anticipating their evidence. He also said that what I had told him supported his contention that had appeared in the newscasts that this case involved "mistaken identity"—the only snippet played by the reporters out of a fifteen minute interview with Gary.

Throughout the remainder of the year, I anticipated the announcement that my case had been presented to the Grand Jury. Their decision would be monumental to my life in that they would either render the decision that there was sufficient evidence to indict me and warrant a trial or insufficient evidence and a "no bill," entirely dismissing the case. I felt very helpless in this situation. First of all, I did not know *when* my case would be presented, I did not know *what* evidence they would be presenting, and neither I nor my attorney would be able to say a word in our defense. All control of the case was in the hands of the prosecuting attorney, including all of the publicity that would surround a potentially sensational trial. I could not present my side of the story until I was in open court. The potential media attention and sensationalism that would accompany such a public trial, I was afraid, would be devastating to me and to my family.

Each time I entered the Rockdale County Courthouse, I would question the security personnel as to whether or not the Grand Jury was still sitting for that month. Whenever they would advise me that the Grand Jury had been dismissed for the month and would not reconvene until the first of the next month, I would call my attorney's office and advise him that another month had passed by and still no indictment. With each passing month, my attorney grew more confident that our case would be dismissed. He revealed that in similar cases, indictments were sought very quickly and the cases speedily handled. He felt that it was apparent that the District Attorney's Office was experiencing difficulties in accumulating quality information and sufficient evidence to seek an indictment.

In early December 2004, I met Gary Moore and he told me he had been in communication with the

Assistant District Attorney in charge of my case and that he now felt we might get "an early Christmas present" in that the Assistant District Attorney was going to recommend that my case be dismissed. Of course, this was very exciting news. I was anxious for the case to be dismissed so I could go back to reclaiming my life. I knew my reputation and integrity had suffered a severe blow, but at least with a dismissal I could begin to truly rebuild my life. Christmas came and went, and there was no word from the District Attorney's Office.

Finally, near the end of January 2005, Gary Moore telephoned me and gave me the disheartening news. He had met with a new Prosecuting Attorney, who had determined that he was not satisfied with the results from the initial investigation of my computers by the Georgia Bureau of Investigation. He ordered that my computers be sent back to the GBI laboratories and reinvestigated. He ordered that the hard-drives be looked at all over again and determine whether or not any new evidence could be located or whether other evidence had been overlooked. Gary told me that the discussion was very impassioned and that strong words were exchanged. He thought that my name may have been heard all over the courthouse. At the same time, Gary felt that this proved that the evidence was lacking to support their allegations. Some of my friends insinuated that it was possible that the investigating officers could be embarrassed that they had made such a big splash in the media by arresting me, but now they were realizing that they didn't really have a case. I really wasn't concerned about the reasons or the motives; I didn't really care. For my family's sake and my own sanity, I just wanted this ordeal to be over.

THE DOCTOR

The months that followed were on occasions difficult for Jim and his family. Gary Moore's steady hand as Jim's legal representative helped Jim remain steadfast in his determination to see things through to the end. This enabled him to not yield to the temptation to work out some kind of settlement with the District Attorney's Office. The church family was also instrumental in giving him support as well as the men's prayer group being a great source of strength for him.

THE OFFICE MANAGER

At every turn, things became more incomprehensible to us. Why would it not end? What made the authorities so determined to find something? Why were facts ignored? Why were moves for dismissal denied? It became more than a person could bear. It appeared to become more than Jim could bear. Only Jim and the Lord know the depths of suffering he endured. And yet, he survived. He survived because he maintained his integrity and faith. He earned the privilege of residing in a city of refuge until the fearful situation finally wore itself out and died.

THE ACCUSED

In April 2005, my attorney, Gary Moore, met again with the Prosecuting Attorney, and Gary was advised that if I would come in and accept responsibility for the images on my computer, that they would secure a suspended sentence and that they would recommend that I not have to serve any further time in jail. When Gary told me this, I was emphatically shaking my head, "No." I was not interested in accepting any compromise or negotiation that would involve me admitting to any responsibility whatsoever. Gary laughed, telling me that he had basically told them that if they had any kind of case that they were to proceed to seek an indictment and that we were prepared to answer them in court. Gary knew what my response was going to be, but he felt obligated to advise me as to what the District Attorney's Office had said.

It appears to me that, although I do not have any evidence to support my contention, a technique that was employed by the District Attorney's Office was to delay seeking an indictment from the Grand Jury in hopes that I would become so unsettled and frustrated that I would come to them seeking to negotiate a settlement, just to end the interminable waiting. Any type of admission on my part, assuming responsibility and admitting guilt, would have had the appearance of a victory on their part and they could publicize that justice had been just as well served as if they had been able to obtain a conviction in open court. Truly, I wanted this horrible situation to end, but I was not going to confess to a crime I was not guilty of committing. To me, to have offered any type of confession or assuming any responsibility would have been tantamount to confessing guilt for everything. My attorney, family and friends all agreed, and although some type of confession would have avoided the spectacle and embarrassment and publicity of an open trial, there was not any consideration given to negotiating any kind of settlement.

Nevertheless, the thoughts of possibly going to trial were terrifying. The possibility of confronting news media questions and their innuendoes was frightening. I was not the least bit shy about privately declaring my innocence of the allegations, but the thought of facing a bank of microphones and cameras was very discomforting. I was too familiar with tabloid-type reporting and I was justifiably afraid for my family's sake. The damage to not only my reputation but the emotional trauma my family would endure was worth almost any price I could pay to avoid.

Consistently, Gary Moore assured me that as time went by, more and more the possibility of a trial became remote. He reiterated that normally any amount of real evidence would have caused the District Attorney's Office to seek an indictment from the Grand Jury quickly. The fact that they had not sought an indictment was indicative that they were realizing that they had insufficient evidence. Furthermore, District Attorneys did not like to receive "no bills" from a Grand Jury and for the most part, only sought indictments when they felt reasonably assured and confident of securing one.

Certainly, as more time passed without an indictment being sought, my confidence grew that eventually everything would work out all right, but it was continually a nerve-wracking experience to simply wait for something to happen. Weeks would pass by without any contact or news from my attorney. Whenever I would telephone Gary or leave him a message, he always responded to my inquiries with great patience and his voice expressing amazing confidence. Sometimes he would express my chances of going to trial as if he were reading statistical percentages, each time diminishing less and less. I continued to question the security personnel at the Rockdale County Courthouse as to whether or not the Grand Jury was sitting. Whenever I was told that the Grand Jury was finished for a month, I would breathe a sigh of relief and thanks, praising God that one more month had passed without an indictment. My prayers grew in confidence as I continued to pray that God would bring about a dismissal without even a presentation of the case going before the Grand Jury.

THE FRIEND

For the next two and a half years, I continually reminded Jimmy that even though the District Attorney might be trying to build a case, there was nothing that existed that they could build a case on. They could not find anything that could possibly connect him to the illegal website. I would try to reassure him that even though I didn't know how, I knew that with God's help and guidance this would all work out alright and that he would be proven innocent of those unbelievable charges.

Our church watched this man put all of his trust in God. Every time Jimmy came to church he held his head a little higher, walked a little taller, as if to say, "Satan, I'm not beaten yet!"

He became an inspiration to many.

THE CHAIRMAN

I watched Jim for two and a half years come to Monday Night Men's Prayer Meetings and he would always have something positive to say. About God. About His mercy. About His grace. About His love.

Never bitter.

Never angry.

THE ACCUSED

At about 4:00 P.M., on Wednesday, June 28, 2006, I received a call on my cell phone from Gary Moore. I was traveling westbound on I-20, returning to my office after finishing a number of legal research requests in a neighboring county. He said that he hoped I was sitting down for he had some great news for me. The day before, Dabney Kentner, Assistant District Attorney in Rockdale County, had signed a document dismissing all of the charges against me. Of course, my first words were, "You're kidding me."

Gary just laughed and said I should be getting my copy of the dismissal in the mail in the next couple of days. I then said, "Thank God. It's really over." Gary said, "Yes, the dismissal is complete and the case is forever over."

I drove on, stunned. I couldn't get my mind to focus for any length of time on any one subject. Is this for real? Is it really over? I wasn't expecting this—not today, anyway. I had hoped this day would come, but I certainly didn't get up this morning expecting it to be today. What if the District Attorney changes his mind? Will they withhold the dismissal like they did back in December 2004? How will I be able to live without this cloud hanging over my head and my spirit? Will I learn to live again? Will people accept me better now? Will those folk who maintain some lingering doubts still be doubtful? Will some people think that I got out of this because of my court connections and that I really was guilty?

I then realized that some of the questions I was thinking were just plain unreasonable and for the most part, out of the realm of my control anyway. But I was having a difficult time realizing that the cloud that had been hovering over me every day for two and a half years was finally disappearing—all because of the Lord. I realized that the only reason I was even alive and sane enough to realize the joy of the dismissal was because of the grace and mercy of my Savior, Jesus Christ. Even with that realization, I felt my emotions being held in check. I had anticipated this day coming for a long time, suffered disappointments along the way, but it was still going to take me some time to accept the fact that the Lord had heard my prayer and the prayers of my family and friends and that the answer was actually here.

I went home and walked into the house, calling for Alison. Alison met me at the foot of our stairs near the front door, and I related to her what Gary had told me. A part of me had debated saying anything until I had actual proof in my hands, but I just couldn't withhold this news from the woman who stood by me without wavering in her confidence and support. She responded to what I told her with a knowing nod of her head. But I cautioned her to wait before telling anyone—we had been disappointed before when the District Attorney's Office had changed their minds and had actually reopened the investigation. What we didn't know was that a copy of the dismissal was even then weaving its way through the postal system.

The next morning, the 29th, I traveled to the Bibb County Courthouse, spending several hours there performing legal research. Early in the afternoon, Alison called me. Unlike the call she had made to me two and a half years before to the same place, she was bringing me good news. The tone of her voice revealed her excitement. An envelope had arrived from the District Attorney's Office and she had opened it to find a copy of a document dismissing all of the charges against me, dated June 27, 2006. Also arriving at the same time was an envelope from the Clerk of Superior Court's Office that held a certified copy of the same document, verifying that the document had been recorded in their office the same day, June 27, 2006. The document stated that the evidence was insufficient to support the search warrant. Ultimately it meant all of the charges and allegations were dropped completely.

Alison said, "Isn't this great?" in a voice that was filled with relief and happiness. It was ironic (some might would call it luck, or fate, or even God's way of showing that He is in control) that in the same Bibb County Courthouse record room, at almost the exact same time, two and a half years before, her telephone call had began the most devastating experience of my life. Now her voice was bringing to me the realization that the nightmare was over and that I could begin to bring praise to the One Who had sustained me and kept me alive to hear this Good News.

The only way that I could respond to what Alison was telling me was to let out a long drawn-out breath and whisper, "Praise God!"

I finally quit dreaming about the color orange.

Always orange.

The dreams eventually faded, but I do remember the last dream I had that featured orange. I dreamed I was in church....wearing a bright orange suit! With an orange shirt! And an orange tie!!

Orange.

Always orange.

THE ASSOCIATE

I knew that the allegations were unfounded and I said as much from the beginning. Jim Reynolds is my friend; that has not changed and that will not change. I like to consider myself a loyal friend, although I may not always do exactly as I should. But if you are my friend and I believe you are in the right, someone is going to have to *show* me differently before I will change my mind. Talk is cheap. Don't talk to me, show me.

And so far, my friend Jim Reynolds is still a true friend to me, my wife, Carla, and son, Louis. We believed he was innocent from the "get go" and don't try to tell us otherwise—you just might bite off more than you can chew!

THE NEIGHBOR

My husband and I always had confidence that a terrible mistake had been made by those who had accused Jim of this horrible act and felt that the truth would eventually come out.

THE OFFICE MANAGER

Life is not fair. It rains on the just as well as the unjust. But God will not allow situations to destroy those who have integrity and faith. He will place them in a city of refuge and allow them to stay as long as necessary.

I think I can speak for Jim and myself when I say that what God has done for Jim, He will do for you.

THE CHAIRMAN

And now the gauntlet is ended. The charges were not upheld and his good name should be returned to him. Through all of this, God taught Jim, his family and his many friends valuable lessons about life and being in submission to God and His Purpose.

The Bible teaches us that Joseph was incarcerated for things he knew he should not do and didn't do. What appeared to be unfairness and fickleness on the part of Jehovah, turned out to be the method that Joseph saved his family from a famine. May it be so with Jim that he can help save many with his story.

The words to part of an old hymn say:

"They that wait upon the Lord shall renew their strength,

They shall mount up with wings as eagles.

They shall run and not be weary, they shall walk and not faint.

Teach me, Lord, teach me Lord to wait."

God's Kingdom and Work, this world and those who know him, are better off because there are principled men like James C. Reynolds who walk among us.

THE SISTER

I never gave in to the thought that Jim was guilty of the charges against him, but that he was a victim of circumstances of today's world. Then came the afternoon two and a half years later after all of this began. The telephone rang and Carl remarked, "Jim's calling," and picked up the receiver. A few seconds later a huge smile appeared on Carl's face and I asked, "Is it over?"

Carl grinned and nodded. "Yes."

My first thought was, *thank you, God*, and I realized my long ago prayer as I had prayed it was answered exactly. I believe God always justifies our faith in Him. He'll never let us down when we place our trust into His promises, for He is as good as His Word.

THE FRIEND

Finally, in June 2006, Jimmy got his dismissal papers in the mail. On the 20th of August, 2006, he spoke in our church on patience and longsuffering. At the end of his sermon, he said, "I've been waiting a long time to do this, so you will have to just excuse me for a minute while I have a jubilee!"

He then placed the dismissal papers on the floor and danced on them. I was blessed with the honors to do the same. Who says God does not perform miracles any more? I was part of this one and if I never see another one, I was truly blessed this time.

Some things that happen in life you may have reason to doubt or wonder about, but not in this case. To see something awful like the allegations against Jimmy happen to a close friend, and then wait…and wait…and wait…and then finally see it proven what you knew all along, is a wonderful and blessed thing. It is something you'll never forget to give thanks to

God for doing. It just goes to show you how much God truly loves us.

The day I danced on those papers with Jimmy will always be one of the happiest days of my life.

THE WIFE

I'm so very glad I stayed with Jim!

THE DOCTOR

Jim and I continued to talk together and pray together from week to week while he kept me completely updated of any new developments involving his case until it finally came to an end. That was a blessed day for all of us. In all of the years I have been a pastor (almost 39 years now), I have not had anyone in my congregation deal with this kind of situation. I do not believe God sent this into Jim's life, but I do believe that it was used to deepen his dependency on the Lord and renew his trust in God's Providence. Jim had always been able to do for himself, but this time he was forced to allow God to work it out according to His will...and Jim just waited and trusted.

CHAPTER 13

THE JAIL
THE ACCUSED

The next three chapters contain my observations concerning various aspects of my two and a half year experience involving the allegations brought against me, plus vitally important data gleaned from my own personal research and studies. This information is being provided to inform you, warn you, encourage you and enlighten you with the means and ideas to help others, even beyond your own family and friends. While some of the information may appear simplistic, the messages they convey could profoundly affect your life and spirituality if prayerfully applied.

The three days and nights I spent in the Rockdale County Jail were as unnerving and demoralizing as imaginable. I had never been arrested before nor been incarcerated, even temporarily, for any reason. The dynamics of incarceration are still very foreign to me and are such that I do not desire further familiarization. Regardless, my experiences and interactions within the confines of a jail facility with both prisoners and guards became the source of several observations of which I wish to share a few. I would not want these observations to be construed as a critique or criticism of the Rockdale County Jail nor of any of its personnel. Rather, my desire is to share with the reader the tremendous opportunities that are available to assist the inmates within jail facilities near you and to turn their lives around. My prayer is that individuals and groups would take the following comments, expand upon them, and take advantage of them to help the souls that lie in jailhouse bunks to discover a new way of living.

First, let me state that I have a tremendously high respect and regard for the American criminal justice system and the individuals who expend their time, talent, abilities and lives working in it. The duties and responsibilities of these law enforcement officials, from the deputy and policeman on the street, to the judges and bailiffs in the courtroom, to the officers and guards in the penal system, are performed, for the most part, as thankless and sometimes dangerous tasks. They are protecting the citizens of our communities by apprehending and incarcerating criminals to prevent the outlaws from committing further crimes. That is part of their oath, putting their lives on the line each day to fulfill that pledge, and all are doing the best that they can with all that budgets will afford them. They also struggle against the political correctness that seems to handcuff the law enforcers more than the criminals.

Thankfully, our legal system, for the most part, works to protect the citizens from being falsely accused and prosecuted. Everyone should applaud and appreciate the policeman who walks the beat in a dangerous neighborhood, the patrolman who drives through our neighborhoods, the judges who have the integrity to enforce the penalties allowed by law and the jail and prison officials who protect us by keeping the criminals off of our streets.

I am not qualified to address the work of police investigators, District Attorneys and judges, nor knowledgeable enough to address every aspect of our penal system. But there is one issue I wish to comment on that appears common nationwide and one that I experienced firsthand—the overcrowded jails.

The fact that many of our jails and prisons are overcrowded proves that our system of justice is working. The more criminals incarcerated, the more safe and protected are the citizens. The only answer to criminal behavior is punishment that fits the crime which helps maintain our society. However, from statistics and my own experience, many of the inmates in our jails and prisons are not first-timers but are repeat offenders. It appears that many of those imprisoned, particularly those involved with drugs, once they are released from imprisonment, repeat their crimes and are more easily apprehended. From the discussions and conversations with prisoners, the majority of them felt that they had nothing much else to go back to except their old lives and criminal ways. Then they end up making the same bad choices and mistakes that led them to jail in the first place, with the same terrible consequences—they are incarcerated away from family and friends.

Could one of the reasons that some of these people commit the same crimes and offences repetitively be because they have not *learned* another way to live? Is it because the only life they know is the criminal life and thus they contribute to the overcrowded condition that beset our community jails and prisons? Are they contributing to the budgetary shortfalls our legal departments endure and our public officials complain about?

While I was incarcerated, I overheard many conversations concerning post-release life. It appeared, for the most part, that I was the only one in my section who had a career and profession awaiting him. I mostly heard my fellow prisoners complaining about the lack of opportunities, particularly in the job market, that awaited them once they were released. I heard many concerns and worries expressed by those who had families and their inability to properly provide for them, outside of a life of crime. I was saddened to overhear one prisoner say that the first thing he would have to do once he was released would be to contact an old partner in misdeeds in order to get some money. All I could see for him was a roundtrip ticket back to the jailhouse.

I discovered that only a few of my fellow cellmates were single; the majority had families. I heard several express concerns for their families' welfare and a desire to provide for them without resorting to crime. While it was good to hear such talk, it was disheartening and discouraging to discover that many of these same men were illiterate and/or unskilled. On several occasions I found myself reading letters and legal documents to fellow inmates. I also answered numerous questions concerning job availability from those who would be soon released. In almost every instance, I could sense the hopelessness and helplessness that pervaded them. For a few, a word of hope and encouragement was all that was needed to bring a smile to their faces.

I do not fault the penal system for the situation. At the community levels, they are dealing with overcrowded conditions and all the dangers and expenses that entails. Plus, many sites endure a shortage of staff and low budgets. While I would support the addition of staff and increase in funds for jail systems from local communities, this will not solve the overcrowded situation. It would only help the community to cope with the problem. I would strongly recommend and suggest that individuals, churches and social groups cooperate with their local jails and together develop more programs to remake the inmates into useful citizens and responsible family men—programs that would not endanger or compromise the judicial system.

If the inmates are remolded into skillful and useful men, the chances are that their incentive to return to a life of crime would be tremendously diminished. With fewer prisoners cashing in their roundtrip ticket to the jailhouse, the problems incurred through over-crowding would diminish proportionately.

Many Federal and State penal institutions utilize some of the following suggestions within their facilities. However, it is not their systems that I wish to address—it's the local institutions that I feel could use the most assistance. I hope the following offers a challenge to many individuals, churches and social groups and provides many opportunities to effectively change lives. If some of these programs are introduced to the local penal systems, it is hoped that the issue of overcrowded conditions would cease to be an ongoing concern.

RELIGIOUS SERVICES AND SPIRITUAL TRAINING

There are many, many hours in a day when the inmates have absolutely nothing else to do but read or, if it's available, watch television. Otherwise, they simply sit around and talk with each other. Unfortunately, too many of those conversations concern when their releases are coming up and the criminal activity they will become involved in. Or the conversations simply contribute to the depression many inmates feel when they talk about family, particularly wives or girlfriends. No matter the topic, the tone of voice is saturated with hopelessness.

Bringing Bible studies along with spiritual awareness to the inmates will cause their outlook toward society and life to change. They need to *learn* that there is a better way to live outside of the drug and alcohol cultures. If their thinking and perspective toward life can be affected, then there is hope that when they are released, they will not revive their life of crime. It would be hoped that they would seek the ways and means to create for themselves and their families a life of respect and integrity—all through changing their minds through biblical values and spiritual regeneration. Through a growing awareness of God's love and plan of salvation, they can change their lives or remain doomed to be a police statistic. Without a change in their thinking, they are destined to repeat their mistakes, over and over again. And that's because they don't know better—they haven't *learned* better. They haven't *learned* that there is a better way to live their lives.

I discovered that many of my fellow cell mates had a religious background, but few maintained any kind of church association at all. They had become disconnected from church life, their morals had become deteriorated or even nonexistent, and their beliefs lacked a firm foundation. Certainly, this would not be the case within every jail, however, many of the inmates would be found to have at least a foundation in religion upon which to build a spiritual awakening.

Having daily Bible studies and frequent religious services would aid many inmates to begin turning their lives around. I have heard the jokes and the ridicule about "jailhouse religion," but I would challenge those who would think such things with, "Where else is it more advantageous to experience conversion than in jail or prison? Where would there most likely to be found people with their minds and emotions more open to spiritual matters—many on a first time basis?" They're in a place of shame and humiliation. They have time to reflect on the bad choices they have made in life. Rather than spending their time thinking about how they could commit future crimes and not get caught, there are many who seek a real change in their hearts and attitudes. Religious services and Bible studies would afford them with the opportunity to *learn* how to make those changes.

I would encourage my readers to contact their local Sheriff's Department and jail facilities and determine what prospects are available. If through spiritual conversion only, some inmates are kept from becoming repeat offenders, then in time, over-crowded conditions would diminish as fewer and fewer inmates return to jail.

BASIC EDUCATION

I wish to encourage educators and learning institutions to seek opportunities to offer classes within the penal system, especially in basic reading, writing and mathematics. I observed several inmates who were without those skills in sufficient measure to function properly in society. Again, in most local jails there are plenty of times available when the inmates have no responsibilities or obligations. Educational classes would not only increase their efficiency and skills but would greatly contribute to their pride and self-esteem. Many of the prisoners would see them-selves accomplishing a goal that would improve their lives and make them better able to contribute to their families' welfare. Certainly one of the basic reasons many people turn to a life of crime is because crime is a means by which they can obtain money—easy money, quick money. Sometimes they turn to a life of crime because they do not have the education or the skills to earn a good income from a secular job. Family pressures and debt will contribute to the decisions they make about life. But taking advantage of educational opportunities while imprisoned would greatly enhance their opportunities to market their trade or skills once they are released.

Vocational and trade training would be a tremendous assistance to the inmates. I discovered that there were many intelligent inmates with the inherent mental ability to learn. Many were more than capable of receiving training in computer skills and other technical fields. Gaining a useful trade or proficiency in a field would afford them the opportunity to earn a professional's income and would go a long ways in deterring them from returning to a life of crime.

In 2006, I heard a radio program concerning a plan developed by a prison in a Southern state whereby inmates were made available to a construction project on a college campus. In exchange, college professors and students, along with professional contractors, trained the prisoners in various skills. Plus, the college gained new buildings at a lower construction cost. The inmates were not only providing physical labor in the construction of a new building, but they were also learning new trades and skills that would enable them to go into a profession once they were released. They were also earning shorter jail sentences for their labors and were afforded opportunities to be hired by the college itself after their release.

Instituting vocational training within the local jails would create an opportunity for inmates to acquire a new skill and escape the criminal world. Along with this, there is a tremendous need for companies and industries who will initiate programs to accept the newly released inmate into their work plans. Tax breaks and other government inducements for these companies would be beneficial. By affording these kinds of educational and vocational opportunities to the inmates, it would be hoped that many of them would develop into useful members of society.

POST-RELEASE MENTORING

From the various conversations and discussions I had with several inmates, the paramount topic and question was, "What's going to happen with me when I get out of jail?" Many of these discussions revealed the total lack of preparedness to deal with the "outside" for most of these inmates. Where was he going to go? Where was he going to get some money? Will his wife and kids be at home? Are they even in town? Have they moved? Is his girlfriend still waiting for him? Is his old job still available? Will he have to look for a new job? Will anyone hire him now? What about all of the bills and debts that will be waiting on him?

There is a tremendous need for individuals who would have conversations and discussions with inmates who are soon to be released back into society. These sessions could lead the inmate into a direction that would benefit him and his family. Information could be shared with the inmate concerning the names of contacts and organizations that are prepared to assist him to make the adjustments needed and to help him get his feet back on the ground.

While counseling and mentoring before the inmate is released is important, following up after they are released is imperative. Knowing how the newly released are adjusting and letting them know there is someone interested in them and helping them will increase their confidence. In every case, getting the inmate back involved with society through families, social groups and churches will help prevent them from becoming repeat offenders and perpetual jail residents.

In a recent conversation with Rev. Clell Eskew of Stockbridge, Georgia, a well-known jail chaplain and prison minister, he revealed that it had been his experience that once an individual is incarcerated for the second time, it becomes very, very difficult to prevent the third and subsequent arrests. He had been involved with jail ministry for a number of years, experiencing the joys of seeing inmates turn their lives around and the heartbreak of seeing inmates not take advantage of the opportunities given to them. Despite the disappointments, he states that his goal remains constant to see the inmates' souls, their lives and their families redeemed. He realizes he is only one man and can accomplish only so much. He strongly advocates that good Christian men and women could achieve great accomplishments for the Kingdom of God by working to salvage as many lives as possible now suffering incarceration in local jails. He fervently believes that through spiritual guidance, educational and vocational training, and mentoring before and after release that the overcrowding that persists in prisons would dramatically decrease.

One last suggestion and thought. If these various programs were to be initiated and utilized in the local penal systems, and the judges were made aware of their existence, the judges would be gaining new weapons to fight crime, repeat offenders and over-crowding in the jails. The judge would be acquiring new options to offer individuals sentenced to serve time for their crimes. The convicted felon could choose between serving their full sentence as allowed by law or take advantage of the various programs available and serve a shorter sentence. Again, the issue of overcrowding in the jail would be silenced and for many individuals, incarceration could prove to be the opportunity of a lifetime to turn their life around. They could become useful and beneficial members of society rather than taking the first step in the vicious and hopeless cycle of repeat offenders.

CHAPTER 14

IDENTITY THEFT
THE ACCUSED

Based upon information obtained from a number of sources concerning the allegations lodged against me, it was determined that a man living in Cincinnati, Ohio, hacked or cracked into my personal computer sometime in the Fall of 2003. He was able to obtain the numbers to one of my credit cards that I had previously used on my computer to make purchases from Amazon.com, Barnes & Nobles Booksellers, and various historical, informational and business related sites. This person then created a child pornography website utilizing an Internet server in Chicago, Illinois, using the credit card numbers he fraudulently obtained from my computer. Apparently, this person began soliciting subscribers to their website by spamming e-mails and sending out computer viruses. The National Center for Missing and Exploited Children became aware of the new site and determined that it was originating from Rockdale County—through my personal computer. Thus began my nightmares.

In orange.

Always orange.

What is identity theft? Simply stated, it is the stealing of another person's name, address, social security number or other identifying information to commit fraud or other crimes without the victim's knowledge or lawful authority. You probably would not know that you have been the casualty of identity theft until you get the bill for merchandise or services you never purchased, or that unexpected call from your bank or some other lender—or the police banging loudly on your door.

Very loudly.

The warning signs that could mean someone has stolen your identity include but are not limited to:

- Denial of credit.
- An unexpected drop in your credit score.
- Calls from collection agencies.
- Normal bills are showing up late or not at all.
- The police are at your door.

Skilled identity thieves may use a variety of low and high tech means to gain access to your personal information. The Federal Trade Commission estimates that 25% of victims of identity theft attributed their identity theft to a lost or stolen wallet or the theft of their mail, including credit card statements, pre-approved credit card offers, new boxes of checks and tax information. The thieves will rummage through trash containers seeking discarded personal data or credit card receipts. They obtain personal information through e-mail solicitations or telephone inquiries posing as legitimate companies. They crack into computers using special programs to record passwords and sometimes unleashing computer viruses. They steal business records or bribe employees at other companies for customer database information. They "shoulder surf" which means watching or listening to you punch in the numbers to your telephone card, your credit card or your bank card.

Once the thieves have obtained your personal information, they can commit a variety of crimes.

- Run up charges on credit cards after calling the credit card issuers to change the mailing address.
- Open new credit card accounts, phone servcies or other utility services and/or automobile loans using the victim's name, date of birth and social security number.
- Steal bill payments from mailboxes, erase what was written in ink and rewrite the check to themselves or an accomplice to be cashed.
- Counterfeit checks or debit cards and access victim's bank accounts.
- Open a bank account in the victim's name and write bad checks on the new account.
- Use personal information to commit unemployment fraud, social security benefits fraud, and even health insurance fraud.

- Obtain loans, even for houses and automobiles.

And then there are the mistakes and crimes committed by companies in which vital personal information has been lost. *YOU MAGAZINE*, in its September 2006 issue, reported that LexisNexus* classified 450,000 consumer files as "breached." Bank of America "lost track" of 1.2 million back-up files. Citigroup "lost" the records of 4 million customers. The magazine also reported that the FTC claims, "27 million Americans have been victimized (by lost personal information) in the last five years, 10 million in the past year alone." More shocking, 25% of those victimized were children.

The front page of the June 25, 2004, edition of *USA Today* reported that an AOL.com employee had sold the e-mail addresses and passwords of 92 million AOL customers to individuals connected to organized crime. The purchasers used the information to solicit subscribers to an online gambling website and later resold the lists to pornographers.

A featured article appeared in the March 21, 2004, edition of the *Atlanta Journal-Constitution*, describing the business of three major companies that re-sale vital information obtained legally through public records via the Internet or through on-site inspection of public records in courthouses and other governmental locations. These records are then collated into lists and reports utilized by a great variety of businesses. The writer illustrated that for $79 he was able to obtain a report concerning a fellow newspaper writer which included addresses for the past 20 years, criminal records including traffic violations, employment history going back 20 years, phone numbers he had used, relative's names, neighbor's names, birth date, education, home values and investments. For $130 the report would include a psychological profile. And for only $39.95 more, all of this information would be rushed overnight to his office.

It should be apparent by now that identity theft is a major criminal activity, although it was not made a federal offense until 1998. Despite the continued public awareness of the potential of being a victim of identity theft, too many people remain careless, particularly with their personal computers. The results of an AOL.com study reported in the October 31, 2004, issue of the *Atlanta Journal-Constitution,* stated that eight out of ten home personal computers are infected with spyware and 85% of users have antivirus software but most do not update on a weekly basis. The study also found that 20% of home users had an active virus in their computers and two-thirds did not have a firewall installed. AOL Chief Trust Officer Tatiana Gau is quoted as saying, "No consumer would walk down the street waving a stack of cash or leave their wallet sitting in a public place, but far too many are doing the exact same thing online."

The October 3, 2004, issue of the *Atlanta Journal-Constitution,* reported that California Governor Arnold Schwarzenegger had signed a law to combat spyware, banning unauthorized installation of spyware on individual computers. The law bans collecting personally identifiable information through keystroke logging, gathering web browsing histories, opening pop-up ads and interfering with a user's efforts to identify or remove the spyware. Under the law, consumers can sue for damages.

The same newspaper issue carried an article by Bill Husted, who characterized spyware as the "latest in a long list of computer hazards" along with "viruses, worms, spam, e-mail and phony websites." He indicated that an Internet surfer would end up "spending more time guarding against and eliminating these threats than they do using the computer as it is intended." He also described spyware and adware as "malicious little programs that monitor your computer usage" reporting back to the program creator. Additionally, these programs can "steal information from your hard-drive" and "even allow the hackers to take remote control of your computer."

Unfortunately, Husted's article was not very encouraging. He concluded by stating that, "this category of computer menace really isn't understood very well, even by the experts, and that despite the increase in attention by law enforcement to cyber-crime. The problem of spyware, like spam and viruses, is not going away."

Cyberspace contains numerous dangers that can attack your computer and cause the lost of vital personal information. The July 17, 2004, edition of *World* magazine reported a virus called "Scob" as the start of a new generation of cyberattacks. "Scob" uses JavaScript to fool users' computers into downloading a piece of software that records their keystrokes.

This could give crooks access to personal information such as passwords and credit card numbers. Microsoft engineers quickly responded to the virus with security updates.

The *Wall Street Journal*, in its November 30, 2004, issue, reported a "bot" virus with which a single person could "hijack" the power of thousands of far-flung computers at one time. These "bot" viruses are used to send out spam, and they make it easy for cybercriminals to cover their tracks. Viruses like these are "notoriously hard to track," the article stated. The popularity of high-speed Internet connections that are always on has also contributed to the spread of the "bot" virus.

The advent of new viruses and other methods of attack on personal computers has also inspired new weapons to combat the insidious assaults. *Time* magazine of September 27, 2004, announced a "Digi-Portals Choice-Mail" program to help fight e-mail borne viruses. For around $40 from digiportal.com, a person receives a software program that only allows e-mails from your address book. If an e-mail from an unknown source is received, it sends back a challenging message. If the e-mail is from a spammer, he won't respond. If the e-mail is from a friend who e-mails infrequently, they will answer. It sets a second mailbox for online shopping convenience. If spammers get your shopping mailbox address (and they will), a new mailbox is set up.

World magazine of October 9, 2004, reported that AOL was offering a "gadget that displays a six-digit code that changes from minute to minute." A user would enter the six-digit code displayed on the devise in order to login to their AOL account and e-mail. The number changes often enough to discourage eavesdroppers and snoops.

Even utilizing new technology and instituting extensive safety measures in all walks of life, your personal information and identity could still be stolen. So what do you do if you become the victim of identity theft?

1. Immediately file a fraud alert with all three credit bureaus.

   • <u>EXPERIAN (formerly TRW)</u>

     To report fraud, call 1-888-EXPERIAN (1-888-397-3742), fax to 1-800-301-7196, or write to P.O. Box 1017, Allen, TX 75013.

     To order a copy of your credit report ($8 in most states), write to P.O. Box 2104, Allen, TX 75013 or call 1-888-EXPERIAN.

     To dispute information in your credit report and marketing lists, call 1-800-353-0809 or 1-888-5OPTOUT or write to P.O. Box 919, Allen, TX 75013.

- ## EQUIFAX

  To report fraud, call 1-800-525-6285, or write to P.O. Box 740250, Atlanta, GA 30374-0250.

  To order a copy of your credit report ($8 in most states), write to P.O. Box 740241, Atlanta, GA 30374-0241 or call 1-800-685-1111.

  To dispute information in your credit report, call the phone number provided on your credit report.

- ## TRANSUNION

  To report fraud, call 1-800-680-7289, or write to P.O. Box 6790, Fullerton, CA 92634.

  To order a copy of your credit report ($8 in most states), write to P.O. Box 390, Springfield, PA 19064 or call 1-800-888-4213.

  To opt out of pre-approved offers of credit and marketing lists, call 1-800-680-7293 or 1-888-5OPTOUT or write to P.O. Box 97328, Jackson, MS 39238.

2. File a police report.
3. Call the FTC Identity Theft hotline at 1-877-IDTHEFT (1-877-438-4338), or TDD at 1-202-326-2502. You can visit their website at www.consumer.gov/idtheft. They can also be contacted by mail at Consumer Reponse Center, FTC, 600 Pennsylvania Avenue, N.W., Washington, DC 20580.
4. Continually monitor your credit reports and immediately close any accounts that you do not recognize as being your own or if you have indication that an exiting account has been compromised.
5. You may need to contact other agencies for other types of identity theft. The local office of the Postal Inspection Service should be contacted if you suspect that an identity theif has submitted a change-of-address form or used the mails to commit fraud involving your identity. If you suspect your Social Security Number is being fraudulently used, you can contact the Social Security Administration at 1-800-269-0271 to report the fraud. If you suspect the improper use of your identity in connection with tax violations, you can call the Internal Revenue Service at 1-800-829-0433 to report the violations.
6. If you have had checks stolen or fraudulent bank accounts set up by an identity theif, contact the following major check verification companies:

CheckRite	1-800-766-2748
ChexSystems	1-800-428-9623
CrossCheck	1-800-552-1900
Equifax	1-800-437-5120
National Processing Co.	1-800-526-5380
SCAN	1-800-262-7771
TeleCheck	1-800-710-9898

Obviously, the best defense is to take precautious measures to make you a less likely target for identity theft. *YOU* magazine offers the following seven suggestions as steps that can be taken to better protect yourself.

- Purchase a cross-shredder and shred every document a person could use to steal your identity. Examples include credit card solicitations, bank solicitations, old bank statements, etc.
- NEVER give your credit card numbers, social security numbers, or other personal information to someone who calls you on the phone and requests this type of information.
- NEVER respond to an e-mail that requests your credit card numbers or social security numbers.
- Check your credit reports regularly and make sure that the information contained within them is accurate. (Consumers can now receive one free credit report per year from each of the three reporting agencies.)

- Check your bank statements every month and make sure they are correct.
- Sign up for a credit watch program.
- Find out if your state has instituted a Security Freeze law to protect people who consider themselves at risk for any reason. (This includes vulnerability for those filing for divorce.)

The May/June 2004 issue of *The Saturday Evening Post*, in an article by Jim Prendergast, declared the first and most important step in self-protection was to install and maintain virus software up to date, recommending Norton and McAfee. Secondly, activate or install a firewall, again recommending Norton and McAfee plus ZoneLabs. Thirdly, delete any e-mail from anyone whose address you do not recognize. Additionally the article suggested:

- Know to whom you give your e-mail address and what they will do with it. Read privacy policies of websites where you enter your address.
- Use multiple addresses. Dedicate one address for business, one for friends, and another "disposable" address for everything else. That way, you can "turn off" the third if it becomes a target for spam.
- Pick a unique address that makes it difficult for the spammer's software to guess. For example, "3johnx5_smith" is more difficult to guess than "johnsmith".

- Report spam to the Federal Trade Commission by forwarding it to uce@ftc.gov, your Internet Service Provider, and the sender's Internet Service Provider.

The August 2004, edition of *The Pentecostal Herald,* carried an article by Keith Braswell entitled "Stay Clean." He recommended seven steps that battle against virus attacks and protect your vital information located in your computers.

- It is not optional, but necessary to install virus-scanning and cleaning software on every computer.
- Most importantly, very regularly update the virus scanning software from the supplier to detect new viruses. Set the software to update every day if you connect to the Internet every day.
- Scan the computer regularly with virus scanning software. Scan any downloaded files and e-mail attachments from the Internet for viruses before opening them. Never open an attachment without knowing for sure it is virus free, even if you know the person who sent it to you.
- Stay informed about the vulnerability patches and security updates of your computer software and apply them as soon as they come out. Set your computer to automatically download these updates and prompt you to do the installation so that you will stay current.

- Turn off automatic processing of e-mail attachments in the Internet e-mail software.
- Scan floppy disks, compact disks, and other storage media,especially those of unknown sources, with virus-scanning software before use.

www.myidentityprotectionplan.com has developed a list of ten practical suggestions to safeguard your identity from not just computer hackers, but from other sources as well. While it's not easy to totally prevent identity theft, significant steps can be taken to reduce your risk.

- Order a copy of your credit report from each of three major credit bureaus at least twice a year. Review and make sure it's accurate. The first place you might see fraudulent activity is on your credit report.
- Place passwords on all of your important accounts. When creating a password, avoid easily obtainable information such as your birth date, your street address or phone number. Use a password instead with a random combination of alphanumeric characters such as 56T4v89.
- Carry and reveal as little personal information as possible. Always leave the card with your social security number (SSN) on it at home unless it's vital to take it with you. Take only the credit card and blank checks you must carry. And when you're on the phone, never

reveal your personal information unless you're absolutely sure you know who you're dealing with. Remember, identity thieves have become quite clever at posing as bank representatives, Internet service providers and even government agencies.

- Safeguard your Social Security Numbers. If your SSN is on your driver's license, you should ask the licensing department for a new license. Never include your driver's license or SSN in the printed information on your checks. In fact, don't give your SSN to anyone unless it's absolutely necessary (such as for filing tax forms). Your SSN is one of your "main identifiers." Thieves can use it to open a variety of fraudulent accounts. You can receive your official Social Security Record by visiting the Identity Protection Plan Website and downloading the Social Security Request form.

- Keep good back-up information about your accounts. Compile a "Personal Identity Check List" just in case your wallet is stolen. With one toll-free call to 1-877-672-3323 you can replace your cards, minimize any potential losses and protect your good credit rating.

- Invest in a shredder. Shred credit card applications you receive in the mail along with bank statements, stock and mutual fund statements, credit card receipts that you don't need and any other financial documents you don't want to fall into the wrong hands. Destroy all old credit cards before discarding.

- Pay attention to credit card billing statements and cycles. Review your credit card bills as soon as they arrive to make sure that the charges stated are really yours. If your bills don't arrive on time, it could indicate that an identity thief has stolen your account and changed your billing address to cover his or her tracks. Be sure to follow up with your credit card company right away.

- Install your Anti-Virus and Firewall Software right away. Firewall programs will keep hackers from acquiring important passwords and data from your computer.

- Consider banking online. If your banking institution offers this service, consider using it. This allows you to monitor your account activity through your computer, track daily transactions and even pay bills. It's much easier for an identity thief to steal your mail than it is to crack a bank's encryption technology. Lock your mailbox to help keep thieves from stealing your mail that does come to your home.

- Do not download files from people you don't know. Opening a file infected with a computer virus could allow a hacker to access your computer and retrieve your personal information. You also should not click on "hyperlinks" (a Website link within an e-mail asking you to click to "find out more") sent to you from strangers.

A growing area of interest for identity thieves is personal medical information. This has one of the fastest rising crime rates in the country with organized crime rings adding a new dimension to the problem. Max Alexander, as reported in the November 2006 edition of *Readers Digest*, offers six ways to protect your medical ID.

- Treat your insurance card like a credit card. Don't lose it or loan it, and don't show it to anyone except a trusted health care provider.
- Watch out for "freebies." Be suspicious of offers for free medical care. Avoid clinics that advertise aggressively, promise to waive co-payments, provide free transportation, or similarly entice you.
- Read the EOB. Carefully review the "explanation of benefits" letters sent from your insurance company, and call about claims for services or drugs that you don't understand.
- Check your benefits yearly. Once a year, request a listing of benefits paid out by your insurer. That way, you'll discover fraudulent payments even if the thief has changed your billing address.
- Request an accounting of disclosures. You have a right under HIPAA to get this document from every health care provider you visit. The accounting will detail what personal

information was released and whom it was sent to. It's a good way to catch and track theft, because any fraudulent medical information will probably be passed along to other providers.

- Review your credit report. If someone has stolen your medical identity and racked up unpaid hospital bills in your name, the charges could turn up on your credit report.

I realize that I've taken up quite a bit of space with this information from various expert professional and governmental agencies and have even been somewhat repetitive in some aspects, but if I can only emphasize into the minds of my readers that it is *imperative and very important*, even *life-saving*, that they must do absolutely everything that they possibly can to safeguard themselves and their families from the seriously horrible and demonically insidious crime of identity theft, then my goal will have been accomplished. Hopefully, no one will ever have to suffer the painful turmoil like what came crashing into my life and the lives of my family, but any crime of identity theft will cause a tremendous amount of anguish, distress and heartache, no matter how big or small.

CHAPTER 15

PORNOGRAPHY
THE ACCUSED

Let me share some shocking and troubling information with you—information that may open
your eyes and cause you to stop and think. Hopefully,
these facts will cause you to become more aware of
the world we live in, the dangers that lurk in our
society, and the necessity to protect your homes and
families with everything you have-especially if you
have the Internet available in your home.

- 12% of all websites are pornographic in
  nature.
- There are 42 million pornographic websites
  on the Internet.
- 72 million people visit pornographic websites
  every year.
- 31% of porn addicts are female.

- Almost 10% of all e-commerce on an annual basis comes from the porn industry.
- The Internet porn industry grosses $20 billion per year.
- There are more porn shops in the USA than McDonald's Restaurants. (*The Pentecostal Herald,* May, 2004)

As you can discern, pornography is a growing threat plus a big business, not just on the Internet but in almost every aspect of our economy and culture. Rich Bordner, writing in the January 2, 2001, edition of *The Lantern*, states that "(pornography) has penetrated the mainstream" of American civilization. It is apparent that sexually oriented materials saturate throughout every level of our society, making it difficult to avoid in even our everyday living and impossible to not be aware of its existence.

While pornographers and sex purveyors are forever creating new and innovative ways and means to distribute their filth, they all fall into one or more of eight major categories as listed in *The Secret War* by Henry J. Rogers (1999, New Leaf Press). I've also included some of my observations.

- <u>Adult Magazines</u>. Not just in adult oriented stores but adult magazines are available in your neighborhood convenience store, not far from the bubble gum and sodas.
- <u>CD's and Video Cassettes</u>. These are rented or sold primarily in adult bookstores, but your local movie rental store could have an

"exclusive" or "special" section devoted to "adult entertainment." For those who wish to be more discreet, there are available mail-order clubs that will rent or sell pornographic movies, delivered to your doorstep in a plain, brown envelope, with generic professional-sounding company names listed as the return address.

- Television. The FCC does not regulate cable in the same way that it does public access stations. Thus, many pornographic movies and even channels devoted solely to pornography are available on cable television. Cable TV is the "ultimate brown wrapper."
- Audio Porn. This includes "900 #'s" and "Dial-A-Porn" telephone calls which have become the second fastest growth market in the pornography industry. Unfortunately, use among underage boys and girls continues to rise every year.
- Strip Clubs. Many in our society have given up trying to control the growth of the strip club industry. Rather than outlawing them and pursuing the criminal element that operate these clubs, government officials are satisfied to regulate them to certain "zones" and collect tax revenues. Then the owners and managers are allowed access to the highest levels of government and are accepted into society as legitimate businessmen (and women). With the promise of making more money in one night than working two weeks

at many other jobs, these places are an easy lure to entrap naïve young girls into a life of sex and perversion.

- <u>Prostitution</u>. With the onslaught of liberal politicians and secularists labeling prostitution as a "victimless crime" and even esteeming the virtue of the "world's oldest profession," combined with the desperation some women find defining their existence, law enforcement has a tendency to look the other way when it comes to prostitution, despite the laws that remain on the books. This currently makes prostitution a growth industry unparalleled in American history. From the woman walking the streets to the high-priced call girl waiting in an even higher-priced hotel, the flesh market is prepared to wholesale the virtue of any woman and rape the integrity of any man.

- <u>Dinner Clubs and Restaurants</u>. A recent marketing ploy to attract new customers to a different type of restaurant is to advertise it as a "family-style" restaurant. In the meantime, the female servers in the restaurant are scantily dressed, many times baring more skin than covering. These "dinner clubs" will advertise their waitresses as being "wholesome," but to any virtuous man they would actually be "embarrassing." Certainly, these are not the type of places to take a family with young children, no matter how good the food may be nor how economical the price. It is heartbreaking to see precious young ladies abused and misused in such restaurants. Their talents, abilities and natural God-given beauty are totally ignored and overshadowed by the exploitation they experience.

- <u>Cyberporn</u>. Hard-core pictures, movies, online chat and even live sex acts can be downloaded and viewed by virtually anyone through the Internet. Sexually explicit images can be found on Web pages and in news groups and are far too easy for anyone of any age to access. What was once only available to a small number of people willing to drive to the bad side of town can now be viewed at any time in the privacy of one's home.

Kerby Anderson exclaimed in the *Probe Ministries Newsletter* (August, 2004), "Pornography is tearing apart the very fabric of our society. Yet Christians are often ignorant of its impact and are apathetic about the need to control this menace. Moreover, Christians must realize that pornography can have significant harmful effects on the user. These include: a comparison mentality, a performance-based sexuality, a feeling that only forbidden things are sexually satisfying, increased guilt, decreased self-concept and obsessive thinking."

The battle is not hopeless. Each family must fight the good fight for themselves, not expecting a secular government to protect them from the advertisements, enticements and evils of the sex industry. Steps must be taken by each individual and their families to maintain their moral values and spiritual integrity. Secularists would call such efforts as "foolish" and "prudish." But which is more important? To have the approval of these people or protect your family members from the incessant attacks of Satan? You are not weaponless. You are not defenseless. There are steps you can choose to protect your family and to fight back the enemy and stem the tide of cultural and societal indifference.

First, parents must teach a wholesome, Biblical view of sex to their children. Helpful aids can be obtained from groups like Focus on the Family and Josh McDowell Ministries. Some excellent books that will be of great assistance includes the series by Stephen Arterburn and Fred Stocker with Mike Yorkey, featuring *Every Man's Battle* (2000, Water Brook Press), *Every Young Man's Battle* (2002, Water Brook Press), and *Every Man's Battle Guide* (2003, Water Brook Press).

Second, we must evaluate our exposure to media (magazines, television shows, rock music) with inappropriate sexual themes. Parents should set a positive example for their children and take time to discuss these stories, programs and songs with them.

Third, pastors and ministers should warn their congregations about the dangers of pornography and instruct them in a proper view of sexuality. Like Joseph in the Old Testament, we should flee immorality which can entice us into sin. Messages should also be given to build a strong Christian home.

Fourth, parents should block cyberporn with software. There are many commercial services as well as special software that can screen and block areas children may try to investigate. These programs will block out sexual hot-spots on the Internet and can detect an offending phrase that might be used in an online chat room. Parents should also try to be around their kids when they are on the Internet and ask them questions about online computing. Extensive late night use may be an indication of a problem. Husbands and wives, agree to work together and say to each other, "Don't worry. I've got your back."

Fifth, individual Christians should get involved with a local decency group which is organized to fight pornography. These groups have been effective in many localities in ridding their communities of the porno plague. The American Family Association (AFA) is one such organization. Founded in 1977 by Don Wildmon, the AFA represents and stands for traditional family values, focusing primarily on the influence of television and other media-including pornography—on our society. AFA believes in holding accountable the companies which sponsor programs that attack family values and commending those companies which act responsibly regarding programs they support.

Sixth, we should express our concern to local officials (through letters and petitions) about adult movie houses and bookstores in the community.

Seventh, if we receive pornographic material in the mail, we should report it to our postmaster and request that federal agents take action.

Finally, do not patronize stores that sell pornographic materials. Consider organizing a boycott and picketing in order to get community attention focused on the problem.

Radical? Revolutionary? Desperate? Some would use these terms to describe what has just been suggested. But when you're fighting for your family and trying to protect them from harm, then what is too radical? Too revolutionary? Too desperate? One of the most dangerous aspects to exposure to pornography in any form is the possibility of addiction and the consequences that could be suffered. According to a study conducted by Stanford and Duquesne Universities, "Two hundred thousand Americans are helplessly addicted to e-porn," (*U.S. News and World Report*, March 27, 2000). In the same magazine, well-known author and radio personality, James Dobson, called Internet pornography the "new crack cocaine."

Dr. Victor B. Clive, as told in Kay Arthur's book, *Sex…According to God* (2002, Water Brook Press), identified a four-phase syndrome common to nearly all of his clients who became addicted to pornography. First, they got hooked early. He wrote, "Once involved in pornographic materials, they kept coming back for more and still more. The material seemed to provide a very powerful sexual stimulant or aphrodisiac effect…" The second phase in sex addiction was the escalation, more and more being necessary to satisfy, just like a drug addict. The third phase was desensitization: "The sexual activity depicted in the pornography (no matter how anti-social or deviant) became legitimized…" in their minds. Following addiction, escalation and desensitization, came the phase where "...an increasing tendency to act out sexually the behaviors viewed in the pornography" developed rapidly.

By now you are probably shaking your head in amazement, but please don't stop reading. I'm not through yet. I must share with you some more disturbing information so that I can encourage you—no, plead with you—to do all that you can to protect your children from the sexually oriented onslaught coming from our modern day media and technology. Tim LaHaye and Ed Hudson, in their book, *Seduction of the Heart* (2001, W Publishing Group), opinionated that "...television and Internet video games have become America's electronic babysitters." They supported this contention by demonstrating how much faster the Internet has grown by comparison to other technological advances. For example:

- It took radio 38 years before it had 50 million listeners.
- It took television 13 years to reach 50 million viewers.
- It took the Internet only 4 years to top 50 million users.

LaHaye and Hudson also reported that with the introduction of WebTV, which marries television and the Internet, that it has the potential "...to become the most powerful media influence in the world."

The same book also carries the results of the Jesuit Communications Project, conducted in Toronto, Canada. Father John Pungente stated, "By the time the average North American child graduates from high school, he or she will have spent 11,000 hours in the classroom, watched 15,000 hours of television, seen 350,000 commercials, watched 40,000 violent deaths, listened to 10,500 hours of pop music and viewed over 400 movies."

Combine this information with the results of a study of video gaming habits of young people, aged eleven to eighteen, conducted by Canadian Professor Stephen Kline of Simon Fraser University in British Columbia, and you have the potential for seriously marred children. Kline reported that:

- Video games have been incorporated into the daily routine of 65% of all households.
- 25% of the young people surveyed considered themselves addicted and admitted they were troubled by their compulsive behavior.
- Internet users spend about 8 hours per week online playing games.
- Parents pay little or no attention to what their children play on the Internet.

The violence and semi-nudity depicted in many of these Internet games have proven to be detrimental in many ways to the lives of young people. Their ability to function socially, emotionally, educationally, mentally and even physically can be severely impaired. And the correlation between many Internet games, pornography and violence cannot be denied. For instance, sexual predators have begun using video game systems, such as the Xbox 360, to target children. The Xbox 360 offers video game players the chance to communicate with each other during game play via headsets through the Xbox Live Service, which works in conjunction with a broadband Internet connection. Some people, however, may use the service to take advantage of children. Georgia Attorney General Thurbert Baker is reported to have said in the October 14, 2006, edition of *The Rockdale Citizen*, that with technological innovations, child predators have started moving away from Internet chat rooms into different methods of communication with children such as the Xbox system.

The main aspect of pornography I wish to address is pornography and your computer. The whole terrible incident recounted in the previous chapters stemmed from pornography, in particular child pornography, being found on my computers. Not because I or anyone associated with my business or in my family had ordered, purchased, asked or traded for any of the images, but because of insidious and consistent cyber-attacks from money-hungry, immoral, demon-possessed, Satan-inspired, evil-personified pornographers.

Before proceeding and for further clarification, I would like to offer the following vocabulary:

- <u>Virus</u> - a computer program that propagates itself by infecting other programs on the same computer. A virus can erase whole files or a complete disk. A virus usually causes pop-up windows or spam. A virus cannot usually be transferred to another computer unless an infected file is traded or transmitted via e-mail.

- <u>Worms</u> - like a virus, can propagate itself, however it can spread itself automatically from one computer to another.

- <u>Spam</u> - advertisement pop-ups that open on your screen automatically, usually from a virus.

- <u>Sporn</u> - is pornographic spam that can be downloaded on your computer accidentally-without you knowing it. It can start with a simple e-mail message about a legitimate product or service you might be interested in. Or it may be disguised as a message from a friend or a business acquaintance. When you check on it, the porn spammer is in and porn images can be put on your computer's hard-drive. One step further and you could end up distributing those images to someone else—all without your knowledge.

- <u>Trojan Horse </u> - is a very general term refer-ring to programs that appear desirable but actually contain something harmful. The harmful contents could be something simple, for example you may download what looks like a free game, but when you run it, it erases every file in that directory. The Trojan Horse's contents could also be a virus or worm which then spreads the damage.

- <u>Crackers</u> - are often mistakenly called "hackers." Crackers are the "bad guys" who seek to "crack" or gain unauthorized access to computers, typically to do malicious things. Crackers might do this by writing a virus, worm or Trojan Horse. Alternatively, they may just exploit weaknesses in the computer's operating system in order to gain entry. Many crackers will install a "backdoor" which allows the cracker to "remote control" your computer over the Internet, such as to distribute child porn. Most crackers have been described as bored, anti-social kids who aren't particularly smart and they just take advantage of well-known existing exploits or the gullibility of the typical Internet user.

- <u>Hackers</u> - used properly, this term refers to an elite breed of "good guys" who are talented computer programmers. They enjoy solving challenging problems or exploring the capabilities of computers. True hackers subscribe to a code of ethics and look down upon the illegal and immoral activity of crackers.
- <u>Anti-virus Programs</u> - are used to check your computer for viruses and prevent their spread.
- <u>Firewalls</u> - are network barriers designed to keep out crackers.

In some cases, viruses will slow your computer down, make it sluggish, or even make it stop running frequently. The worst case scenario is a computer cracker gaining control of your computer and information. There are four major means that porn spammers attack your computer and infect your computer with a porn virus or worm.

- <u>Harvesting</u> - Spammers have programs that "harvests" or collects e-mail addresses from chat rooms, news groups, guest books and lists of those who visit Websites. Then they "blast mail" a virus to your computer that will cause pop-ups to appear advertising their porno products. Certainly, the greater majority of recipients will simply delete the pop-up, totally uninterested. But the spammers are not concerned about those that delete. If the spammer blasts out a thousand e-mails and only one person is curious enough or addicted enough to visit the Website and possibly purchase a subscription, the spammer is making money—lots of money. And usually the spammer is advertising multiple sites, enhancing the possibilities that the spammer is going to arouse someone's interest.

- <u>Website Attachments</u> - As described previously, I viewed a legitimate medical Website to only later have pornographic pop-ups to appear on my computer screen. Pornographers seek to attach links to their porno sites with other Websites, even legitimate ones, in order to potentially attract new subscribers. Pornographers will pay thousands of dollars to obtain research information that reveals the top visited Websites and then they'll spend even more money developing ways to link their porno sites to the top visited Websites.

- <u>E-mail Attachments</u> - Pornographers utilize many different methods to secure e-mail addresses, and when they gain that information, they will send an e-mail, usually with attachments that when opened, reveal images from the porno site. The e-mails are many times disguised, appearing to be from a legitimate advertiser or company. Because of the prolificacy of information warning Internet users to not open unrecognizable e-mails, the spammers developed programs that if the e-mail was opened, but not the attachments, a virus would still invade the computer. Later, the spammers developed programs which would regenerate itself every third time a computer was turned off and on. For each new development to block and protect the computer from these type of infections, the spammers became that much more proficient in bypassing the safeguards.

- <u>Search Words</u> - Pornographers will constantly seek out surveys which reveal the top search words being used by Web searchers on the Internet. Then the pornographers develop links to their Websites that appear in the lists whenever that search word is used.

In a survey for the months of September and October of 2004, as reported by <u>www.Mikes-Marketing-Tools.com</u>, over 40% of the top 500 Key

Search Words for that period were sexual in nature. Of course, the porno people would be automatically linked to all of those words in huge numbers, but porno sites can be found to be listed in the most innocent of search terms. Because of the time of year, the report depicted many of the top search words involved Halloween and the upcoming Presidential election, but still the greater majority of the search terms revealed links to porn sites. The top ten search words for that period were "yahoo," "weather," "mapquest," "e-bay," "google," "Paris Hilton," "games," "Halloween," "music" and "hot-mail." The word "girls" was number thirteen. "John Kerry" and "President Bush" were numbers seventeen and eighteen respectively. Sadly, the highest numbered spiritual search term was "religion," coming in at 341st place.

The porno spammers are very sly and slick, however. If you were to search for the "white house" you would assume that you would receive a list of Websites concerning the home of our U.S. President. You would, but among the listings would be a link to whitehouse.com., which if you click onto it, you would not find pictures of the White House in Washington, DC, but rather pictures of a white house apparently occupied by only nude females.

I know of a woman who sat with her children researching "Disney Parks" in anticipation of a trip for her family. As she looked at the links displayed, she saw one that advertised "Disney Parks Promo," or so she thought that was what it said. Thinking she would be looking at a site advertising price discounts and travel deals, she opened the link to find that what she thought was a "promo" was actually "porno!!" There before her eyes were the familiar Disney characters explicitly displayed in various sexual positions and activities. The spammers had so lettered and configured the word "porno" to look like "promo." It can only be imagined the antics this poor frantic woman went through trying to delete the images and at the same time protect the eyes of her children.

One of the most dangerous and effective weapons in the pornographers arsenal is the use of a Trojan Horse as defined earlier. A Trojan Horse, much like the huge, hollow wooden horse sneaked by the Greeks into the fortified city of Troy, of *Iliad* fame, is a malicious, security-breaking program that is disguised as something benign. For example, you download what appears to be a movie or music file, but when you click onto it, you unleash a lethal program that erases your disk and sends your credit card numbers and passwords to a stranger, or lets that stranger hijack your computer to commit illegal activity.

Trojan horses are executable programs which means that when you open the file, it will perform some action or actions. In Windows, executable programs have file extensions like "exe," "vbs," "com," "bat," etc. Some actual Trojan horse file names include "dmsetup.exe" and "LOVE-LETTER-FOR-YOU.TXT.vbs." Trojans can be spread in the guise of literally anything people find desirable, such as a free game, movie, song, etc. Victims typically downloaded the Trojan from a www. or FTP archive, or just carelessly opened some e-mail attachment.

Trojans usually do their damage silently and unseen. The first sign of trouble is often when others tell you that you are attacking them or trying to infect them!

www.sophos.com reported on August 1, 2003, the story of Julian Green, 45, of Devon, England, who was cleared the previous July of thirteen charges of making indecent images. Green spent nine days in prison and three months in a bail hostel, similar to an American halfway house, before having the charges dismissed of storing child pornography in the hard-drive of his computer. Computer forensic consultants identified eleven Trojan Horses on his computer, "capable of carrying out actions without the user's knowledge or permission." Green described his experience as "nine months of hell." In the same report the story of Karl Schofield was related. He was acquitted of charges involving child pornography when a Trojan Horse was found on his personal computer. Sadly, Schofield was not acquitted before being attacked and beaten by a group of vigilantes while awaiting trial.

Graham Cluley, Senior Technology Consultant with Sophos Anti-virus, states, "Some Trojan Horses have the ability to take 'remote control' of your personal computer...A remote hacker can view what you are doing, take over your keyboard, steal information and even upload files to your computer, if they wish."

Realizing the dangers inherent in Trojan Horses and desiring to avoid infection, read the following suggestions. Some of these will be repetitive in association with viruses listed earlier but the emphasis

here is on the malicious Trojan Horses and the tragedies that can occur if your computer was to become
infected.

- Never download blindly from people or sites
  which you aren't 100% sure about. Like
  the old saying, don't accept candy from a
  stranger. If you do a lot of file downloading,
  it's often just a matter of time before you fall
  victim to a Trojan.
- Even if the file comes from a friend, you still
  must be sure what the file is before opening
  it. Many Trojans will automatically try to
  spread themselves to friends in an e-mail
  address book or on an IRC channel. There is
  seldom reason for a friend to send you a file
  that you didn't ask for. When in doubt, ask
  them first, and then scan the attachment with
  a fully updated, anti-virus program.
- Beware of hidden file extensions. Windows by
  default hides the last extension of a file so that
  innocuous-looking "Susie.jpg" might really
  be "susie.jpg.exe"-an executable Trojan! To
  reduce the chances of being tricked, unhide
  those pesky extensions.
- Never use features in your programs that automatically get or preview files. Those features
  may seem convenient, but they let anybody
  send you anything which is extremely reck-
  less. For example, never turn on "auto DCC
  get" in IRC, instead always screen every single
  file you get manually. Likewise, disable the

preview mode in Outlook and other e-mail programs.

- Never blindly type commands that others tell you to type or go to Web addresses mentioned by strangers or run pre-fabricated programs or scripts (not even popular ones). If you do so, you are potentially trusting a stranger with control over your computer, which can lead to Trojan infections or other serious harm.

- Don't be lulled into a false sense of security just because you run anti-virus programs. Those do not protect perfectly against many viruses and Trojans, even when fully up-to-date. Anti-virus programs should not be your frontline of security but instead serve as a backup in case something sneaks onto your computer.

- Don't download an executable program just to "check it out." If it's a Trojan, the first time you run it, you're already infected!

One other weapon utilized by the porn spammers is "SPIM." As reported in the February 2, 2004, issue of *Time* magazine, "SPIM" is the new word for spam sent via Instant Messaging. 582 billion Instant Messages were sent in 2003, and that adds up to a lot of "SPIM." A sample of "SPIM" would be to receive an Instant Message from "COOLKID0492." When opened, the message would read. "Hey, I'm a 19/f/ca. Wanna come check me out?" The Web link attached would be to a porno site featuring a Web camera. Of course, these can be easily stopped. All

Instant Message programs give you the blunt option of blocking individual users or receiving Instant Messages only from people on your contact lists. ICQ is a program that lets you filter messages even more selectively by blocking all Web links (most porn "SPIM" has links in it) or certain offensive words. The "SPIM" problem may not be totally solved with this program but it is a step in the right direction.

There are many suggestions of ways and means that anyone can utilize to protect themselves and their families from the dangers that lurk on the Internet and in particular with pornography. It would be difficult to give every strategy that could be employed but there are some simple and common sense methodologies that can be implemented. Prayerfully consider these and others that you may find and God will help you to protect the most valuable possessions you have— your soul and the souls of your children.

Keith Braswell, in the technology sections of the February 2004 and March 2004 editions of *The Pentecostal Herald*, offers these suggestions for families and their computers. First, be accountable. For e-mail, every child should be accountable to a parent and every parent should be accountable to their spouse. Know their logins and passwords. Make them aware that you will be checking on them. Train them that we should always be accountable to God and each other.

Next, be safe. Use a firewall that allows you to control what information is allowed to come in and go out. Subscribe to Internet providers that have services that help you filter unwanted content.

Beginning acrobats learn their acts first with a safety net. Even experienced construction workers are required by their employers to wear a safety harness. You are doing your family an injustice if you do not provide a safety net of protection. The day will come when they will, hopefully, practice the principles you have taught them in their own families.

Importantly, be knowledgeable. Would you leave a loaded gun just anywhere with a toddler in your home? Careful gun owners know where the gun is at all times and know that it is safely put away until needed. Be informed of the various ways the enemy can lay down traps to catch you and your family unawares. Be careful of allowing your child unrestricted use of tools that you know nothing about. Just as a careful parent will watch what their child is checking out from the library, we must know what the proper uses of our technical tools are and provide guidance.

Place computers in a public area of the home where others can easily view the screen. By keeping the screen within view of the rest of the family, the user is accountable to everyone. Also limit use. It is a good practice to limit the use of the Internet to certain hours for children. (Some firewall packages allow for access to be limited to certain hours). Have an "open door policy" regarding login information. Children may have their own e-mail address only if they understand that the parent is allowed login username and password, and may check up on them from time to time. Spouses should not feel uncomfortable for each other to have login information to their Internet accounts.

Keep a log of computer activity and set up access to allowed sites. Software can be purchased for this, but even without buying additional software, some things can be done to increase accountability. Check the "history" of the Internet browser to know what kind of sites are being visited on any computer. Be selective in the sites that children are allowed to view and create lists of the allowed sites. Firewalls allow the user to open up only certain sites to the home network. If the home network is connected to the Internet, parents or guardians should have the ability to restrict certain sites. It is better to work with an allowed list than a restrictive list because this allows complete control. It takes more work and effort to maintain, but it is much safer, Braswell concludes.

On a lighter note, computer guru Bill Gates once said, "Thou shalt use a Windows PC to do thy work and it will be good." But all computers, no matter the brand name, are vulnerable to plagues of Biblical proportions: viruses that bring down entire networks, e-mail worms that replicate at lightning speed, Trojan Horses that hide inside otherwise innocent programs, hackers and crackers that take over computers, and more. Thus, thanks to PC World Computer Center and the archeologists who unearthed two stone tablets from a garage near Stone Mountain, Georgia, we have help that can deliver us from these evils. So, with a little help with the interpretations from our brothers and sisters in the PC Security Choir, we present the Ten Commandments of PC Security.

I. REMEMBER THY ANTI-VIRUS SOFTWARE AND KEEP IT UPDATED. It's not enough to have the software installed (if you don't have an anti-virus package, stop reading right now and get one); you also need to keep up with new viruses as they emerge. "Your anti-virus software is only as good as your latest virus definitions set," says Kelly Martin, senior product manager for Symantec's Norton Anti-Virus.

II. THOU SHALT NOT COVET THY NEIGHBOR'S ATTACHMENTS. You get a message from a friend with what looks like a cool file attached, so you click on it. Next thing you know, you're Typhoid Mary, spewing out infected e-mails to everyone in your address book. That's how the Sobig.F worm spread—and it happened so quickly that millions of copies got out before the anti-virus companies could update their databases. "Never trust an e-mail 'from' address," adds Chris Wysopal, director of research for security consultants @STAKE, "And never open an attachment without verifying it was sent by a trusted person, and they meant to send it to you."

III. AVOIDETHBOGUSFILEDOWNLOADS. Be wary of any Web site that requires you to download software to view a page, unless it's something familiar like a Flash plug-in or Acrobat Reader. The file may contain a virus, a Trojan Horse or some auto-dialer that calls pay-per-minute numbers via your modem and racks up huge charges. "Do not install software via the Web unless you are absolutely sure what it is and that you trust the company you are downloading from," warns @STAKE's Wysopal.

IV. SMITE SPYWARE AND POP-UPS. Like Trojan Horse programs, spyware secretly installs itself when you download software like file-swapping applications; it tracks your movements online and delivers ads based on where you surf. Pop-up ads can also exploit security flaws in Internet Explorer, like the recent Qhost Trojan that hijack users' browsers after they viewed an ad on the Fortune City Website. Fortunately, there are tools to protect you. Some anti-virus software and security suites also stop spyware and pop-ups in their tracks.

V. THOU SHALT FOIL SPAMMERS. Unsolicited commercial e-mail is more than just a nuisance; it's also a major source of virus infections. In fact, some versions of Sobig are designed to turn infected PC's into zombie machines that can be used to send spam. A good filter helps trap the nasties your anti-virus software might miss.

VI. KEEP THY OPERATING SYSTEM PATCHED. E-mail-borne worms and other scourges like to exploit security holes in your software-namely Windows and other

Microsoft programs. These days Microsoft issues so many critical updates to fix these flaws that many users ignore them. Don't. Last January (2004), the "Slammer" worm exploited a vulnerability that Microsoft had fixed more than six months before. But thousands of infected computers— including some at Microsoft—didn't have the patch installed. Run the Windows Update program once a week and whenever Microsoft issues a warning. "Until we see automated patch management software, users will simply have to stay up to date," says Thor Larholm, senior security researcher at PivX Solutions.

VII. MAKETH A RESCUE DISK AND KEEP IT HANDY. When things go bad, a boot or rescue disk is your first step to recovery. At minimum, you'll want to put the basic elements of your operating system on a floppy disk or Zip media, so you can bypass the hard disk at start-up. A better idea: Use your anti-virus program to create a rescue disk you can use when your system gets infected. Label it with a date and store it near your system where you won't lose it.

VIII. BE NOT TAKEN IN BY FALSE CLAIMS. There are more hoaxers than hackers on the Internet, and more bogus "e-mail-virus-alerts" than actual viruses. Even real virus threats are typically blown out of proportion by the media. A phony warning could cause you to delete harmless files and then forward the message to others, clogging e-mail servers and causing virus-like damage in the process. When you get one of these e-mails (or see yet another breathless news story), check it out first. Type the name of the alleged virus into a search engine to see if any of the major security vendors have issued an alert, and visit the virus hoax pages at F-Secure and Hoaxbusters.

IX. HONOR THY FIREWALL. A firewall is like a bouncer for your computer—it checks every ID at the door and won't let anything in or out until you give the thumbs up. So a hacker can't access personal information on your hard drive, and a Trojan Horse keystroke logger (a stealth program that monitors the characters you type) can't steal your passwords and transmit them over the Net. The best deal is to purchase an Internet security suite that combines anti-virus, fire-wall, ad blockers, spam fighters and other useful applications.

X. MAKETH BACKUPS AND KEEP THEM HANDY. Simply put: Back up your data files at least weekly (daily, if you're running a business). Even if you fall victim to a virus or hacker attack, you'll escape with only minor damage. Fail to keep a recent backup though, and you'll go straight to hell—at least, that's how it will feel!

In conclusion of this chapter I have some wonderful news for everyone. Remember the eight major categories of pornography listed at the beginning of this chapter? (If not, just flip back a few pages.) Well, there are Scriptures to combat and to resist each and every one of those areas. Whether you just see these areas as you live your daily life or whether you are fighting a battle in resisting them as temptations, these Scriptures are mighty weapons for any warrior of the Lord's!

- <u>MAGAZINES</u> - "For all that is in the world, the lust of the flesh and the lust of the eyes and the boastful pride of life, is not from the Father, but is from the world." (I John 2:16)
- <u>CD's AND VIDEO CASSETTES</u> - "For by these He has granted us His precious and magnificent promises, in order that by them you might become partakers of the divine nature, having escaped the corruption that is in the world by lust." (II Peter 1:4)
- <u>TELEVISION</u> - "If you do well, will not your countenance be lifted up? And if you do not do well, sin is crouching at the door and its desire is for you, but you must master it." (Genesis 4:7)
- <u>AUDIO PORN</u> - "Let no unwholesome word proceed from your mouth, but only such a word as is good for edification according to the need of the moment, that it may give grace to those who hear." (Ephesians 4:29)

- <u>STRIP CLUBS</u> - "Keep your way far from her, and do not go near the door of her house." (Proverbs 5:8)
- <u>PROSTITUTES</u> - "Do you not know that your bodies are members of Christ? Shall I then take away the members of Christ and make them the members of a harlot?" (I Corinthians 6:15)
- <u>DINNER CLUBS AND RESTAURANTS</u> - "Finally, brethren, whatever is true, whatever is honorable, whatever is right, whatever is pure, whatever is lovely, whatever is of good report, if there is any excellence and if anything worthy of praise, let your mind dwell on these things." (Philippians 4:8)
- <u>CYBERPORN</u> - "For why should you, my son, be exhilarated with an adulteress, and embrace the bosom of a foreigner? For the ways of a man are before the eyes of the Lord, and He watches all his paths." (Proverbs 5:20-21)

CHAPTER 16

CONCLUSION
THE ACCUSED

It was in early February 2004. Outside was typical Georgia winter weather—rainy, cold, windy, dark, gloomy—and the weather matched my mood and feelings perfectly. I was late getting home from working in a county courthouse, driving in the miserable mist and spray that surrounded my automobile. The sun had been set for an hour, though the whole day had been like nighttime, with the sun hidden behind the clouds. As I turned into the subdivision where I lived, my headlamps and the streetlights both seemed incapable of penetrating the darkness. The streets appeared morbid, lonely and abandoned. Only dimmed, flickering lights appeared in the windows of my neighbor's houses, but they were brighter than the light emanating from my home. My house was as dark as the blackest night, darker than midnight in a cave. No lamps. No lights. No life.

My wife had not yet returned home from her chores and shopping. The "cottage" was empty—my office staff had already left for the day. Even my dogs, Jeb and Mosby, could not be seen. They were probably buried under the straw in their shelter under the back porch, escaping this miserable winter's evening.

I was physically beat, having traveled to several courthouses during the day. But I was emotionally spent as well. Only days ago, my picture had not only been prominently displayed on the front page of the newspaper with all of the lurid details of my arrest, but the story had been broadcast on many radio stations plus my arrest picture had been flashed around the world on CNN and other television stations. Throughout that day, as on the previous days, I had avoided meeting the eyes of anyone. I had probably not spoken to half a dozen people, avoiding conversations as well. I simply went into the deed record rooms, performed my search work and left. In and out, as quick as lightning.

I had found it particularly difficult going into the courthouses that day, especially whenever I would anticipate running into people I knew and had not seen since my arrest and release. How many times was I going to have to defend myself? How many times was I going to have to repeat the tale? Was I going to be believed? Would I have to see the incredulous looks on some people's faces? Was I going to see a smirk and hear a "Sure, innocent until proven guilty, right?" Would I ever finish "explaining" the whole ugly episode? These questions and more were constantly running through my head and depressing every attempt of mine to be positive and optimistic.

There were times when I entered a deed record room and noticed the averted looks and the timid glances from some folks that made me simply want to scream out—"It's not what you think! I'm not a pervert! I'm not a pedophile! The charges are not true! Just because a person is accused and arrested for a crime does not mean that they are automatically guilty! There is absolutely no evidence to substantiate the allegations! You are judging me guilty 'til I'm proven innocent!'" But I couldn't. I remained silent with my head down and my eyes on the floor. I was ashamed because of what had happened. I was humiliated not only for my own sake but for the sake of my family as well.

I wondered if any of my family members were being hammered with questions and insinuations. I wondered if my children would deem it necessary to separate themselves from me. I wondered if my wife would stay with me. One of the conditions of my bond made it difficult for me to see my grand-daughter, and I wondered if I had seen her for the last time. I wondered if there were strangers looking for my house, even right now, hoping to harm me or my family or vandalize my home.

I knew, as I got out of my car and walked into my house, that I should be feeling safer, more secure, because I was home. I was within the safe confines of my shelter away from the world. But those kinds of comforting feelings, so familiar from the past, were not to be mine on this evening. They just weren't there. The anxiety flooding my mind was tormenting my soul. My anguish was ripping and tearing at my heart. My despair was gripping and strangling my spirit. I was feeling desperate. Depression had consumed me.

I climbed the stairs and walked into my "library." That's what everyone in my family called the room that I had renovated and converted into my own study. It had been Rob's bedroom, and when he moved to college and work in another state, I painted it and installed floor-to-ceiling bookshelves along two walls. I placed my father's old desk and swivel chair in there along with two Queen Anne library chairs. With a ceiling fan swirling and a desk lamp emitting a soft light, it was my place of escape. I could work on my business accounts, write letters, pay bills and read a good book, all in the safety and privacy of my "library." And there was that special spot in front of one of the library chairs where it was comforting to kneel down and talk with the Good Shepherd.

However, entering into the library tonight brought no sense of relief or escape. Among all of my other emotions I was enduring, I also felt a sense of bitterness begin to rise within me. Misery had become my constant companion, and I felt angry that my life had spiraled downward so dramatically. I sat down behind my desk, leaned back in my chair and closed my eyes. The questions began gallivanting through my head again. What in the world am I going to do? What all are people thinking? I hope no one is calling me names but who am I kidding? This world loves a scandal, and the media lives to report malicious stories. The gossips are burning up the telephone lines and the e-mails with, "Have you heard what happened to Jim Reynolds? Well, let me tell you. They say...."

Just how long is this whole thing going to last? How long is it going to go on? How many more embarrassments can my wife and mother and children and sister and friends stand? The publicity from my arrest alone was certainly mortifying enough to all of them. So how in the world can I ask them to endure more?

I leaned forward and put my head down, my fist pounding the top of my desk. My frustrations poured out of me as the tears rolled down my face. The low rumbles of thunder, the noise of the wind, and the sound of the rain outside my window were drowned out by the moans and groans that pulsated from my soul. I was so sick of all of this. Why can't it just end? Why can't it just be over with? How much longer was this hammering going to go on inside of my head?

My mind reeled when I contemplated the future. Through my tears, the only things I could see were troubles and gloom. Will there be a presentation to the Grand Jury? I didn't know, but from all I had heard it appeared the District Attorney's office was determined to make some kind of case against me. But would they get a "true bill" or not? Would there be an indictment? Neither I nor my attorney could be present at the Grand Jury and we couldn't present our side of the case, so more than likely the District Attorney would present everything that would heavily influence the Grand Jury to issue an indictment. So a trial seemed most likely. What a horrible thought that was! But then, would I be forced to compromise? Would I be forced to negotiate a plea—pleading guilty to charges that I knew were not true? Would I—could I—and my family endure the media frenzy and publicity that a trial would bring?

I just couldn't see it. I just didn't think that I could go through a trial, and I didn't want to see my family endure such an ordeal. It wasn't fair to any of them. They were totally innocent and to have to suffer because of what was happening to me was categorically unfair. I didn't want them to sustain any more hurt than they had already. I didn't want them to suffer any more embarrassment. Enough was enough and all that they were suffering was my fault. Dear Lord, I prayed, I would give anything to be able to alleviate all that they have endured. I would give anything to be able to ease the pain they have suffered so far and I would certainly do anything to keep them from suffering any more.

A thought flashed through my mind and I turned and picked up my telephone. I called a doctor I knew. He was cognizant of my situation and was very solicitous as to my health and feelings. I told him I needed some extra strong sleeping pills. I had not been sleeping very much at all since getting out of jail and when I did sleep, there were those dreams, nightmares in orange.

Orange.

Always orange.

He expressed concern about my heart and the possible interaction between the other drugs I was taking. I pressed for something to help me and he finally relented and agreed to call in a prescription to my local pharmacy. I immediately drove to the store and picked up the medicine—a thirty day supply of Temazepam. And in my mind, I felt I had found a solution should a trial become imminent—I just wouldn't be there.

I drove back home, arriving to find the house still dark and empty. I walked back into my library, sat back down behind my desk, pulled out the bottle of pills and stared at them, contemplating all of the possibilities. The little white capsules were to help me sleep for six to eight hours. Thirty pills taken at one time, how long would I sleep? 180 hours? 240 hours? Forever?

At least long enough that District Attorneys and reporters and men in orange would never bother me again.

I never took even one of those capsules. In fact, I placed them in a desk drawer where they remain to this day. Although the expiration date has long passed on what I thought was a solution to my problem, it remains a reminder of how far God has brought me and how the actual and real solution has never stopped working. The final solution was not in pills or in death, but it was in life.

"...I am come that they might have life, and that they might have it more abundantly." (John 10:10).

The pressures, feelings, emotions and the dynamics in my life and in the lives of my family and friends affected by the accusations, allegations and charges brought against me and the subsequent media publicity were unbelievable. I don't know that I could enumerate or name them all much less detail and describe what they all felt like. Probably any emotion or feeling that you could name or describe was experienced by either me or someone in my family, especially during the early months of this episode. Only when it appeared that there was not going to be a presentation to the Grand Jury for an indictment by the District Attorney's office and the possibilities of an actual trial diminished greatly did I begin to recover my equilibrium. Certainly, when the dismissal was issued and was actually in my hands, many of the aftereffects of my depression began to dissipate, and I was able to totally recover my self-confidence. Although it still took me several more weeks before I realized that this whole ordeal was finally and irrevocably over, the final realization was evidenced by my "dance of jubilee" at my local church when I announced my dismissal to the congregation several weeks later. Some may have thought that was out of character for me, but my exhilaration for what God had done for me overwhelmed any reticence on my part.

As it is only through God's mercy and grace that I am on this side of that trial of my life, and I am able to share with many what the Lord taught me through that ordeal, this brings me to the whole purpose of this book. Well, actually there are several important and vital purposes that must be revealed. These were hard lessons and some people may not understand the values of these lessons until they themselves at some time facing as difficult of a situation as I faced. I would not want to have happen to anyone else what has occurred in my life, but after all was said and done, God revealed to me that I was to serve as an example to many others and that the victory I and my family won is only an illustration of the kind of victory God wants to bring to every person who will trust Him and put their faith in Him.

One purpose of telling my story is to remind everyone that the Lord will not place any more on your shoulders than you can bear. Whatever may be going on in your life that causes you difficulties and pain, you CAN make it because God knows exactly how much you can take.

"There is no temptation taken you but such as is common to man: but God is faithful, who will not suffer you to be tempted above that ye are able: but will with the temptation also make a way of escape, that ye may be able to bear it." (I Corinthians 10:13).

You can never really know just how strong you are and your ability to endure hardships in the Lord until you have to endure situations that test you and you face battles that your abilities and talents are incapable of producing victory. When your strength is tested to the utmost, then you will find out what you are made of. I can't say that I ever thought I could endure what I went through from January of 2004 to June of 2006, without either losing my mind or destroying myself. But God sustained me from the beginning to the end and brought to light the lesson that He knows you and me better than we know ourselves. He has the "riches of glory" available to our beck and call if we will only subjugate our pride and determination "to do it ourselves" and let Him lead us "through the valley of the shadow of death" and bring about His perfect will and purpose in our lives.

Another purpose that this ordeal reveals is that there will be trials in life that God will use to demonstrate His power, love and grace by delivering us *from* the problem or battle. But then there will be those kinds of difficulties and trials in life that God will demonstrate His power, love and grace by delivering us *through* the problem or battle. God could have delivered me *from* my computer problems but He didn't. He delivered me *through* my computer problems. The Lord could have delivered me *from* being arrested but He didn't. He delivered me *through* my arrest. Jesus could have delivered me *from* being jailed and being threatened with death but He didn't. Jesus delivered me *through* the jail and the death threats. My Savior could have delivered me *from* depression and the thoughts of suicide but He didn't. He delivered me *through* the depression and preserved my life. He displayed His power and love and grace by delivering me *through* my trial, *through* my problems, *through* my difficulties, so that,

"...after that (I) had suffered for a while, (Jesus would) make (me) perfect, establish (me), strengthen (me), settle (me)." (I Peter 5:10).

And the question can be asked—just how did God demonstrate His power *through* this trial? How did God prove His love *through* this problem? How did God show His grace *through* this ordeal?

Jesus Christ used, what I like to call, "The Magnificent Seven." He utilized seven different sources to display His power, love and grace. It's perfectly logical that He used seven sources for we are taught from the Scriptures that seven is God's perfect number. And since the trials we go through are "...to make you perfect...," these "Magnificent Seven" sustained me and let me know that God was going to be with me all the way.

And you should be happy to know that the "Magnificent Seven" are not my exclusive domain. They are available to each and every one of you. Some of the seven may be stronger or more dominant in your life than others but any Child of God, any person who yields their lives to fulfilling the call of God upon their lives, can find these "Magnificent Seven" working in their lives and helping them to overcome the difficulties and problems that beset them. No matter what your circumstances, no matter your situation, no matter what you are facing, God has many resources like the "Magnificent Seven" to let you know that He is right there, that He loves you, and that He is working to make your life a fountain-head of praise to His glory.

Consider this also. Should it be that your situation is not one He'll deliver you *from* but it is one that He'll deliver you *through*, look around you and you'll see the "Magnificent Seven" all around you and you'll find that God is speaking directly to you to let you know that He is right there all along!

- The first of the "Magnificent Seven" is family.

Proverbs 19:14 says in part, "...and a prudent wife is from the Lord." The word prudent in the Old Testament language means "to cause to act wisely," "to understand." Throughout the whole course of the allegations charged against me, my wife, Alison Virginia, acted wisely and with great understanding. From the genteel and wise manner in which she conducted herself when the investigators came barging into her life and home and through the many ways she expressed her understanding of my needs for the remainder of the ordeal, the Lord used her to display His love. She constantly stood by me, demonstrating her devotion by the simple holding of my hand and giving me cards like the one that read,

> "You've been a thoughtful, loving husband
> From the very start,
> That's why I'll always give you
> All the love I hold within my heart."

Even when I knew she was filled with fears and uncertainties, she let her wisdom from God be her guide, and many a time she was the one who led me through the dark hours of my despair and depression with the bright light of hope that burned from her faith in God.

My gray-haired mother, Lorene Reynolds of Crawford, Georgia, sent me numerous cards, notes and letters. She often expressed in them and to others that she felt hopeless in her desire to help me, but her prayers, thoughts and words of encouragement were sometimes the only things that helped me to make it through one more day. In the many cards that she sent me, she would always underline the important words she wanted me to be certain to read, and she always added her own words of comfort along with those printed in the cards. Her constant reiteration was "I love you very much" and "I'm praying for you."

And she was always giving me puzzles to solve, written on the cards. She would note a Scripture reference at the top or the bottom of the card but she wouldn't write down what the Scripture said or quote it. She was always making me look them up. For instance, one reference was Nahum 1:7, "The Lord is good, a stronghold in the day of trouble; and He knoweth them that trust in Him." Another one was Psalm 62:8, "...God is a refuge for us." She knew that I would receive more strength by reading the Scriptures for myself rather than her writing it down. And she was absolutely right.

One of her favorite phrases to write was "I'm always here for you." And she sent me the words to one of her favorite songs written by Rev. Don Johnson:

"Alone and brokenhearted, filled with despair,
No one to help you with the load you bear.
Giving up is not the answer, quitting is never right,

The Lord can come to you and break up your
  night.
Just whisper Jesus, oh, Jesus,
There's power in that name to set you free.
There's never been a name so sweet,
Lift up your eyes toward Him and whisper His
  name."

Then there were my children and my granddaughter, who unfailingly kept faith and confidence
in me. AJ and Rob interrupted a well-earned vacation
trip to be here when I needed them. AJ's wife, Maggie,
and their daughter, Misty Jane, always showed love
and concern and consistently asked about me. And
they are now being blessed with another child, due
in June 2007. My two daughters, Joy Myers and
Jenna Reynolds, were constantly in touch with me
and telling me I was going to make it. Their inquiries about the case were always filled with love and
concern.

I will never forget coming home one day, several
months after this whole affair began and Alison telling
me there was a message on the answer machine from
our girl, Virginia Etta, living in Charlotte, North
Carolina. She was attending Morningstar Ministry
School and also teaching there. She wasn't able
to communicate with us very often because of her
classes and work, but she took the time on this day
to call and leave me a message that she had felt God
had wanted her to share with me. Her message was
a prayer, a prayer for deliverance and she prayed
fervently on the phone, passing through to me the

power that she must have felt. I played the message over several times because it had come to me just when I needed it most.

I thank God for my sister, Beverly, and her husband, Carl Martin. You talk about sticking up for your "little brother," they both did it with a lot of moxie, tenaciousness and fortitude. Bev's notes, letters and "thinking of you" cards were always timely and said just the right things. Her "we are all behind you" and her "we love you very much and pray everyday for a quick and complete resolve for you," were just the right tidings I needed to perk me up when I felt the blues.

As with all families, our lives can be so busy and so full of cares that it is often easy to forget one another. That's why I was especially touched when my teenaged great-niece, Courtney Martin, took the time to write a very thoughtful, mature and encouraging letter. She expressed her love for me and my family and that she was praying God would keep His hands on me. She wrote, "I'll be here for you (and) even though I'm young, I will do everything in my power to help you out any way that I can." She concluded with "...I'm sticking by your side all the way."

Among too many families, the relationships between former spouses can be tedious, uncomfortable and strained. I counted myself very fortunate in that my former wife, Jennifer, never criticized or insinuated anything untoward throughout the whole ordeal but on numerous occasions expressed support and appreciation that I did as much as I could to insulate our children, Joy and Jenna, from any overt publicity. Although I'm sure concerns and worries filled her thoughts over the possible consequences to her new business, she encouraged me by her kindnesses whenever we met.

I was additionally fortunate that Alison and I, along with her former husband, Jim Rolling, and his wife, Carol, had developed a strong, mutually supportive bond because of the children, AJ, Rob and Virginia, over the years. Jim Rolling and Carol openly and poignantly expressed their respect and appreciation for my relationship and support of the children since Alison and I had married. When they learned of the charges against me, they were both quick to declare their disbelief and offered to assist Alison and me in any way that they could. They both said that none of the children had ever expressed concerns over inappropriate behavior on my part and that they returned our unqualified love.

In my critical time of trouble and depression, my family gathered around me and were ready to defend me like the warriors of Israel in the Old Testament and like the Minutemen in the American Revolution. God used them to show me that He cared and that He was with me and by my side "all the way."

- The second of the "Magnificent Seven" were my neighbors.

Gary Moore proved himself to be more than just my neighbor and my attorney. He was concerned for my physical and emotional welfare and did his best to help us above and beyond the call and duties of law. Throughout the miserable and endless tribulations involved in securing my release, he was constantly in communication with members of my family and with Dr. Jerry Patterson, never failing to quickly and promptly return every phone call and inquiry, continually updating them and advising them of every development. Throughout the two and a half year wait for further action concerning my case, he consistently expressed confidence that everything was going to work out all right and that he was prepared for any contingency. His wife, Irene, was a tremendous help in that she was able to talk with our other neighbors and calm their fears in the midst of all of the disruptions that occurred. She staunchly contended that things were not as they were depicted in the media and that she was confident her husband would clear the matter up soon.

Linda Baker is my champion. She and her husband, Ed Baker, a lifetime law enforcement officer, were constantly checking in on me and Alison, making sure we were safe and secure. Linda's boldness and outspoken disbelief of the charges against me during the news broadcast made my family and friends so very proud of her. During the interview she adamantly declared that the accusations against me were false. I was told that when some of my friends heard what she said on television that they cheered and clapped for her. Her very inspired and exceptional defense brought a smile to my face and through her, I was shown that God could influence Kings, Empires and District Attorneys.

- The third of the "Magnificent Seven" were my friends.

It has been said that you will find out who your true friends are when times get rough. Not only do you find out who your friends are, but additionally you discover that there are people who care for you that you didn't realize you meant anything to them. Throughout the whole two and a half year "day of trouble" I went through, I was constantly and pleasantly surprised and truly happy at how different ones rallied around me. They listened to God and encouraged me when I needed it most. I can't possibly name each one and their gifts to my life during this time, but I do pray that God will repay each and every one of them multiple times.

I'd have to admit that I did not always have an appreciation for all of the cards that I had received in years gone by, but the cards received during this period of my life touched further and deeper into my heart than many other things have in the past. Cards affected me in many different ways, like the one from my long-time friend, Joe Patterson, sent to me that simply said, "I'm glad I know you." John and Kay Black sent one that said, "Just wanted to remind you how unique and special you are to God and so many others." I received a special note from James and Betty Downs that recalled how Alison and I befriended them when they moved to Georgia and stood by them, but now that I was going through "…a trying time…it is our turn to stand with you and Alison in prayer until deliverance comes…"

I received innumerable e-mails, like the several from Jeff Massey of Oklahoma, and phone calls expressing support for me and my family. I cannot recall them all but one telephone call remains outstanding and remarkable in my memory. Leon Walton, Jr. is a longtime friend of my family, our relationship extending back to his grandfather, Rev. J. T. Payne. Leon called one day and he told me he stood ready to do whatever it took to help me. He said that if I ended up having to go through a jury trial that he would "…gather as many people as I can and we'll make signs and we'll march around the courthouse during the trial until they let you go. The media people need to know that there are people who love you and support you."

The variety of things that people sent to me and my family to encourage us would fill a Sears-Roebuck catalog. Books, cards, flowers and gifts would appear serendipitously but would never fail to encourage and uplift. Fighting depression as I was, God used my friends to bring to me the strength I needed to maintain my integrity and not lose hope and faith.

A friend of mine from many years ago, Donald K. (Joe) Patterson, a prolific poet and storyteller in his own right, wrote a unique poem for me entitled:

MY SPECIAL FRIEND

I met this special friend of mine
Over forty years ago,
And that he would be my friend this long

How was I to know?
At first I only saw him
At youth camps in the summertime,
The times we had and the things we did
Should have been a crime.

If you got into a towel fight with him,
His 'rat-tail' would turn the tide.
And if I came in and saw him in action,
Brother, I would turn and hide.
He was also good at baseball
But he batted left-handed, you see,
And I always played right field
And he would always knock it over me.

By the time we both got married
Our friendship was true-blue,
We put on many plays at church
For that's what we loved to do.
His family and mine became close friends
And we all still are today,
But to think he would do something wrong
Well, there is just no way.

We've been through too much together
And known each other too long,
There is no question in my mind
For our friendship is way too strong.
His father was called 'Sarge'
A man who was truly great,
And his mother treated me like family
Which I still greatly appreciate.

Oh, there have been the hard times
When we were not as strong,
But in those we encouraged each other
And helped each other to get along.
There were many times when he'd just talk
Just to have someone to hear,
And in return he'd do the same for me,
Those times are so precious and dear.

He and I have a standing agreement
That involves a pillow in hand,
But it can't be shared with others
Only we can understand.
We've talked of a yellow Corvette
And a trip to Old Mexico,
Yet in all the years I've known him
We never took the chance to go.

But we're still friends through thick and thin
And we will always be,
So if you want to see what real friendship is
  like
Look at my friend and me.
We've known each other all of these years
Through good times and bad,
We've cried together in those hard times
And laughed when we were glad.

Though many things have come our way
Together somehow we've stood it all,
He's shown the mark of a life-long friend
And there's just not a higher call.

They will stick with you no matter what
All the way to the end,
And when it's all over I'll be blessed to say,
'Thank God, I had him as a friend.'
                                        (August 2006)

The Lord not only used longtime friends to brighten my day and to bolster my faith, but He used some new-found friends also. I'm talking about the members of my "posse." They sent me several letters, encouraging me "...to pray and everything will work out for you." In another letter, they wrote, "God is in control and He will set you free." They recalled our Bible study sessions, my "preaching" patience, and their appreciation for my prayers. Despite having lost contact with them, I have continued to pray that God would work in each of their lives and that God would bless "my posse" and their families.

- The fourth of the "Magnificent Seven" are co-workers.

Another resource that God used to keep me within His arms of love were the people who worked for me, especially my office staff—Robin Criswell, Melissa Koscinski, Denisha Keith (now Patterson) and Ashlee Forrest (now Heffington). They were all very loving, loyal and supportive, but never invasive in their inquiries. Though they have all gone on to bigger and better things, their kindnesses will never be forgotten.

Then there were the folks in the courthouses. Several of those that I worked with in the deed record rooms-lawyers, title searchers and other legal researchers-did not always know how to approach me and were reluctant to ask very many questions, not knowing how I would receive their inquiries. But the fact that many remained cordial and friendly, like Robert Diggle, and continued to accept my presence with grace and professionalism despite the allegations, were a tremendous help to me to keep my business going and keep my mind busy with work.

The Lord also used the professional staff in one of the courthouses. Elaine Hall serves in the Henry County Clerk of Superior Court Office in McDonough, Georgia. She represented all of the other ladies and staff in the Clerk's office in a letter she sent to me expressing sorrow for the allegations, knowing "...they are not true..." and concluding with "...our prayers and thoughts are with you and your family." Having sentiments such as these coming from those who I had dealt with only in a professional basis for a number of years was a source of great encouragement and hope.

- Fifth, there were fellow church members.

Church can be a source of help or a source of woe, depending on the character and personalities of the people who make up the congregation. I was blessed to attend Faith Tabernacle in Conyers, Georgia and to have the members of that congregation rally around me and let God use them to uplift me and my family.

From the cards sent by members like the one from Jay Barwick that said, "You are an inspiration to me and I thank you for your faithfulness," to songs like "In The Garden" sung by Sean Peacock; "It Is Well With My Soul" sung by Summer Neal; "So That I Could Still Go Free" sung by Johnny Peacock; "Firm Foundation" written and sung by Leon Walton, Jr.; they all became fountains of hope to my thirsty soul and they allowed me to drink my fill.

And there were the members of the Men's Prayer Group who would take the time to listen to me and offer words of encouragement, wisdom, knowledge and prayer; men like Ricky Patterson, Johnny Mathis, Ed Horne, Steve Rosser, Rev. Clell Eskew, Lee Eskew, Dr. James Harper, Steve Hardy, John Elrod, Ashley Neal, Michael Patterson and Rev. Richard Shorter. God used all of them to keep the light of hope burning in my soul and spirit.

- The sixth of the "Magnificent Seven" was my Pastor.

I first met Dr. Jerry A. Patterson, introduced earlier in this narrative, in the 1960's when he and his wife, Sally, were married. Later we attended the same college and then he went to Athens, Georgia, where he pastored Whitehall Pentecostal Church. My family and I began attending there in 1971 and he and I began a close friendship that has extended to the present. Without a doubt, although I know I've never done anything worthy to deserve his friendship, he went above and beyond the call of pastoral duty to help me through the difficulties depicted in these pages. While he aided me in his role as a Pastor and counselor, even more so he aided me as a friend.

From the moment I called him about the seizure of my computers until the time the dismissal was issued, Dr. Patterson befriended me, counseled me and pastored me. When there were times that I could not express my feelings, he would quietly listen then talk to me in the strong conviction of confidence in God that he not only preached but lived on a daily basis. One of the signs of true friendship is the capacity to sit in each others presence in total silence and not feel uncomfortable. We passed this test on numerous occasions.

I've often heard it said that if an individual were to end up saved that they would need to be within touching distance of a Pastor. When my sanity and maybe even my very life and salvation were on the line, my good Pastor was there to keep me from losing sight of my hope. From the words he spoke in the pulpit to his exhortations in private, he consistently spoke to my spirit as God led him.

- Lastly and certainly not the least of the "Magnificent Seven," is prayer.

Prayer should not be a one-sided talk from just us to the Lord. Prayer is supposed to be a conversation—we talk and He talks to us, too. For years it has been my habit to read the Bible in the morning and to pray in the evenings. As this case dragged on, I found my favorite spot to pray was to kneel at a Queen Anne chair located in my "library." That became my spot to pray. That became my altar. That's where I felt God was waiting to meet with me and talk with me. And it was through my prayers and the prayers of my family and friends that God gave me the strength to endure *through* the trial of my faith.

Initially, when I prayed about the accusations against me, I prayed for deliverance and for deliverance, right now. Immediately. I didn't want any delays. I wanted to see some action. I became adamant that the charges were to be dropped immediately if not sooner, then my life would go back to normal. But after I was arrested and I suffered embarrassment and humiliation caused by the sensationalized media exposure, I began to pray simply to have the strength to endure just through the day. My despair, depression and hurt caused me to focus on myself so much that I was missing what God was trying to do. Eventually my prayers changed, and that's when God began moving.

For about the first twelve months after my arrest, I prayed fervently for deliverance. I prayed for a miracle. I wanted a miracle and I wanted it right now. I prayed that the ordeal and trial would end, if not for my sake because I was unworthy, then at least for the sake of my family. "Please, dear Lord, let this suffering end now. Quickly, Lord. Even so, come quickly."

Then one evening at a Men's Prayer Meeting, I began to tell the Lord that I was tired—oh, so tired. I had been battling my fears and depression for a year, and there did not seem to be any more progress toward a solution than there was a year ago. The District Attorney's Office had not presented my case to the Grand Jury. My computers had been returned to the GBI for re-examination. My attorney could not offer a time-frame in which to expect closure. There just did not appear to be any end in sight, and I was just plain tired. I could not seem to get the energy and mind to feel like I could endure much more. Just what do You want to get out of this, God? If all things are to be for Your glory, how in the world are You going to get any glory out of this mess? I've tried to be faithful. I've tried to be hopeful. I've not complained. I've not hinted that You are to blame for this situation. I've not even asked why? Just tell me what else I'm supposed to do. Where do I go from here? I don't have any answers. I don't understand at all. I just don't have any idea what to do anymore.

It was then, with all of my heart, that I began to pray Luke 22:42—"...nevertheless not my will, but thine be done." Understand, that's a very difficult and hard prayer to pray. It is difficult to give up control over your life. I realized that I had not done a very good job concerning the case against me so far, but I knew I was tired of being "guilty 'til proven innocent." I had to surrender my will, my control, my life, totally and unreservedly, withholding nothing. My prayer became, "God, here's my life. Use it for your purpose and glory. Whatever it takes for You to receive all of the honor and all of the glory and all of the praise in what's going on in my life, then I'm willing. Here and now, whatever it takes, whatever time it takes, whatever will give You the highest praise and glory, then I want to do it. Whatever I must do, whatever I must endure, if it brings to You what You want, then I'm Your servant."

My prayer became harder to pray for I felt in my spirit that God was demanding more of me than I thought I was capable of giving. But I had passed the point of desperation. I needed relief for my sorely depressed mind and spirit and the realization that I was totally hopeless and helpless within myself in this situation caused me to reach deeper into my heart and mind and cry out for His mercy and grace. So I prayed…

"Lord Jesus, if the highest praise to You will come from delivering me from this case, then let it come. Let deliverance come. If You want me to go through a trial and if going through a trial will serve Your kingdom, then I'll endure it. Let the trial come. If it's Your will that I go back to jail because that will serve Your purpose, then I'm willing to go. Let the jail time come. If going to jail means that I would be killed, but my death would serve Your cause, then I'm willing to go. Let it come, Lord."

This was not easy to pray at all. But I realized that if the Lord let Peter and Stephen and other great men of God, certainly much greater men than me, suffer pain and agony and even death in order to serve His purpose and cause, then who am I to think that I'm so special that I shouldn't have to go through anything less? Then I realized that if the Lord had chosen me to suffer, no matter to what extent, then I should feel honored that He had chosen me. Jesus must see in me that I'm worthy to suffer and that it will serve His kingdom. How could I do less when He had suffered the shame and humiliation and the death on the cross for my sins?

Rather than focusing on death by sleeping pills and ending my life, my purpose changed to living for Him and fulfilling His purpose. No matter what it cost me, even my life, I had to fulfill my destiny in Him. It's hard to say, "even if it kills me," but once I became unafraid of death and unafraid of what the authorities could do to me and unafraid of what the future held in store for me and looked to the One Who held the future, my depression left. I began living—*knowing*—that whatever was going to happen was going to fulfill His will and purpose for my life. Whatever came my way was going to serve His kingdom and His cause. My confidence grew by leaps and bounds, and the dark despair that had over-shadowed me began to immediately dissipate.

From that moment, I began living Job 13:15, "Though He slay me, yet will I trust Him..." My whole outlook on my life and the case against me changed to one of hope and confidence.

Certainly, I still occasionally suffered fearful thoughts and even had some more nightmares.

In orange.

Always orange.

The enemy doesn't stop attacking just because a victory has been won. The enemy continued to seek ways to connive his way into my thoughts. But the Lord had brought me into a new dimension of realization and it was this and I'm repeating what I wrote earlier. The miracle of deliverance that God worked in this case against me was not that He delivered me *from* my trial, but that God delivered me *through* the trial—all the way to the end.

As you review the "Magnificent Seven" that God used as resources to demonstrate His power and love and grace to bring me *through* this most shocking and horrific trial, I hope you can find your own place as one of God's resources. You may be so blessed that you are not currently facing or enduring any difficult times. But surely, you know someone who is! I pray that you would realize that God can use you as one of His "Magnificent Seven" to encourage and spread faith to someone who is suffering right now. You may not be a Pastor, but you may fit in the category of family member or neighbor or friend. If you know of a relative, friend or acquaintance from work or a fellow church member who is currently going through a tough time, contact them.

Now.

Right now.

Maybe you know of someone going through marital difficulties or facing financial problems or a serious illness. Just a phone call or an e-mail or a card or a simple pat on the back may be the only thing standing between them and pure desperation. Be sensitive to God, pray that He'll lead you to someone who lacks, watch out for those in need and observe the people around you every day. When you discover, and you will, that someone is going through a difficult time in their lives, seek God's purpose and to learn what to say and how to say it. I encourage you to do this because I found that there were several people who wanted to speak to me about my difficulties, but were incapable of articulating their support appropriately. There were some who thought they were encouraging me but were in fact embarrassing me and were even offensive. I'm sure my own depression dominated my reaction in these instances, but with careful prayer and consideration, the right words will always come forth and will serve the purpose that is needed.

I encourage each one to take time out from their busy schedules and set aside certain hours during the week to concentrate on those who could use encouragement from you. Trust me, the day will come when you'll need someone to listen to God about your needs!

To fulfill the purpose that God placed in my life is the goal of this book. My purpose, the reason God delivered me *through* this terrible trial and problem rather than deliver me *from* it, was so that I could tell you that no matter what you may be facing in life right at this instant, putting your faith and confidence in the Lord Jesus Christ is the very best thing that you can do. Understand, He may not deliver you *from* your dilemmas. He may choose you to be an example to others and deliver you *through* your problems.

You may be facing severe health problems right now. Physically, you are hurting and life is unhappy because of your pain. God can heal you and deliver you *from* your illness or disease. That would be a tremendous miracle. But it would be just as great of a miracle if He chooses to deliver you *through* your illness or disease. It may be that the illness you are now enduring may actually last you for the rest of your life. You may have a disease that eventually will take your life. Does that mean that God is any less of a healer? No, certainly not. But it may serve His kingdom for Him to simply keep you all the way to the end of your life, then delivering you from your illness and pain by bringing you into eternal life. Can you let God choose you for such an honor, knowing that it would be serving His cause and His purpose? It's not easy to surrender ourselves like that, but if you've surrendered to His will and His way, God will use your integrity throughout your sickness to touch the lives of lost loved ones and to encourage family and friends.

You may be enduring a serious marital situation or dilemma right now. You and your husband/wife are suffering difficulties and differences that seem insurmountable. You may be dealing with infidelity or physical abuse. God is able to deliver you *from* this problem and heal the wounds that have been inflicted. He is the "Counselor" and can resolve the differences and keep the family together. But then, it may be necessary to submit yourself to His will and let Him deliver you *through* your difficulties. He is the "Prince of Peace" and can give you peace of mind and emotional stability to work out our differences. In the end though, you could still suffer the break up of your marriage and even endure a divorce. You and your spouse could wind up going your separate ways for the rest of your lives.

Assuredly though, you can make it. If you've surrendered to His will and to His purpose, without reservations or any questions, and your serving His cause with all of your heart, soul, mind and strength, even your separation and divorce will be used by Him to serve His kingdom and His glory. The purpose may be to enrich someone else's life that you don't even know right now, but God holds the future. And God can do all of that!

You may be dealing with serious financial difficulties right now. Maybe you're facing unemployment. Bills are piling up. Debts are out the roof. Bankruptcy seems to be staring you in the face. You're dreading the possibility of homelessness and the break-up of your family. God can deliver you *from* your situation. He could let you win the lottery or a rich uncle could leave you a fortune. You could discover a map leading to buried treasure or you could find a pot of gold at the end of the rainbow. But then, God may so deem you worthy that He will deliver you *through* your financial woes to the point that you may live the rest of your life totally unable to ever rub two pennies together. You could actually end up dying dead broke. You may never become a billionaire. You may work hard every day for the rest of your life barely making ends meet. But does that make God any less of a deliverer? NO, NO, NO! What He can do is deliver you *through* your financial difficulties—with peace of mind, gentleness, self-respect, integrity—and make you such an example of God's power and love and grace that your influence could reach from sea to shining sea.

My message is simple. If God delivered me *through* the problems I faced beginning in 2004, then certainly He will deliver you. Even though I certainly do not feel that I deserved His miracle of deliverance, I am thankful He chose my situation to demonstrate and exhibit His power and love and grace and glory. Whatever the circumstances you may be facing, accept God's will and whether He delivers you *from* your problems or He delivers you *through* your problems, to God be the glory!

Remember! God's love comes in all colors—even orange!

Heavenly Father;

I praise You for Your name's sake, Jesus, and I proclaim Your mighty Name. I praise Your Majesty and Glory, Your Love and Grace, Your Mercy and Your Power. I pray for those reading this right now that if they are being battered by life's depressing dilemmas, that You will lead them to accept Your Will and that You will show them Your delivering Power either *from* their problems or *through* their difficulties. And I pray they accept Your Will and Your Purpose to further Your Kingdom and Your Cause.

I also pray for those who know of others who are facing difficult times and distress. I pray that they will seek a way to offer comfort and consolation to those in need and that they will listen to Your Voice and offer to those who are suffering words of hope and encouragement.

And I pray for Your Blessings and Salvation upon all who read this and keep Your loving arms around them all.

In the Precious Name of Our Lord and Savior, Jesus Christ,

Amen and Amen.

AUTHOR'S NOTES

I want to personally thank you for obtaining this book. My hope, trust and prayer is that it will prove to be inspiring and will assist you in your walk with God. In the troubling and dangerous times in which we live, it is beneficial to read something GOOD and not just because this was written by me, but because the inspiration came from the Lord and the book you hold in your hands has been prayed for by many, many men and women who desire to see God lifted up.

The story you're about to read is a true story. The narrative, for the most part, follows events that occurred in my life from January 2004 through June 2006. As the story unfolds, you will find different viewpoints being presented by the "Cast of Characters" listed later on. These "characters" will present their perspective, feelings and emotions of the events that transpired. It is hoped that by reading what others thought of the events and by observing their reactions, you will find that you know of others that have suffered similar tragedies in their lives and you will discover ways to react that will help that person.

Also included are chapters that concern the jail and prison system and how you can become involved with assisting those who can still be helped to change their lives. The severe and tragic problem of identity theft and the constant menace and threat of pornography and what you can do to protect yourself and your families from these vicious attacks are also addressed.

The major thrust of this book involves three things. First, God is to be praised to the Highest for His miracle of deliverance, not *from* my problems but *through* my problems. Secondly, while your life may be at this time trouble free, you're probably aware of people who are going through some hard times. This book is to help you know *how* to help them and what to do to become God's assistant in the Kingdom. Thirdly, Dr. Jerry A. Patterson is a Licensed Clinical Psychologist who is aware of the limitations of psychological assistance but knows the unlimited resources and power of God. His commentary will greatly lift you up and enhance your walk with God.

I would ask of you one request though. Would you, when you finish reading this, pass it along to someone that you may think might need it? My goal is to lift His Name up on high and to encourage and sustain as many people as possible. By giving this to another person you will be spreading the Good News even further.

My prayer is that God may bless each and every one of you.

James C. Reynolds
November 2006

Guilty 'til Proven Innocent
Order Form

You may fax, send by postal mail or use PayPal to place your order.

Mail: **Fax:**   **PayPal:**
Agape in Orange   770/786-6743   www.agapeinorange.com
PO Box 81483
Conyers, GA 30013

Item	Quantity	Price	Sub-Total
Guilty 'til Proven Innocent		$20.00 (Includes taxes, shipping & handling)	
		TOTAL	

Delivery Information:

First Name:_____Last Name:_____

Street Address:_____

City:_____State:_____Zip Code:_____

E-mail Address:_____

Phone Number:_____Extension:_____

If you have any questions, please call
770/784-8251 or email jimreyscv@aol.com.

AGAPE IN ORANGE MINISTRIES, INC.
"Pointing the Hurting to Helping Hands"

This ministry has been established to assist pastors, of any denomination and of all faiths, to locate assitance for their membership. Pastors are often called upon to be a 'Jack of all Trades' to their membership and are sometimes faced with situations that are beyond their education and their life experience. Agape in Orange Ministries is there to provide the Pastor with assistance, information and direction to help their members.

For instance, if a Pastor has a woman attending his church who is coming out of the adult entertainment industry, Agape in Orange Ministries can assist the Pastor by putting him in touch with 4SARAH, Inc. 4SARAH, Inc. is a minstry that focuses on helping women come out of the adult entertainment world and earn a respectful place in society.

If the Pastor needs assistance in counseling from a professional, Agape in Orange Ministries can place him in contact with professional clinical psychologists who can offer assistance and guidance.

Maybe a Pastor is faced with a family who has practical difficulties such as having enough food. Agape in Orange Ministries can put them in touch with one of the chapters of Angel Food Ministries.

From legal and medical assistance to psychological profiles, Agape in Orange Ministries is there to help the Pastor to better serve his congregation. Pastors no longer need to feel helpless or become stressed from having to deal with situations that are beyond their expertise. Agape in Orange Ministries will show that God's love comes in all colors – even orange!

"WAR HORSE"

The "War Horse", shows a horse in the heat of battle…a battle already won. Seeing the fierceness in the horse's face as he's running, we can feel that our own battles seem the most heated and fearful. But, Jesus has promised He can be, and is, the Victor over anything and everything – no matter how frightening!

This picture can bless anyone who battles fear or anyone who would like a visual reminder that the final victory will be the Lord's! We can look at the painting and be assured that the fight is indeed the Lord's and breathe a sigh of relief and peace. Give Him your battle!

"War Horse" note cards and prints can be ordered @ www.agapeinorange.com.

Printed in the United States
128032LV00001BD/88-288/P